Inclusive Music Histories

Inclusive Music Histories: Leading Change through Research and Pedagogy models effective practices for researchers and instructors striving either to reform music history curricula at large or update individual topics within their classes to be more inclusive.

Confronting racial and other imbalances of Western music history, the author develops four core principles that enable a shift in thinking to create a truly intersectional music history narrative and provides case studies that can be directly applied in the classroom. The book addresses inclusivity issues in the discipline of musicology by outlining imbalances encoded into the canonic repertory, pedagogy, and historiography of the field. This book offers comprehensive teaching tools that instructors can use at all stages of course design, from syllabus writing and lecture planning to discussion techniques, with assignments for each of the subject matter case studies. *Inclusive Music Histories* enables instructors to go beyond token representation to a more nuanced music history pedagogy.

Ayana O. Smith is Associate Professor of Musicology at Indiana University, USA.

CMS Emerging Fields in Music
Series Editor: Mark Rabideau, University of Colorado, Denver, USA
Managing Editor: Zoua Sylvia Yang, DePauw University, USA

The *CMS Series in Emerging Fields in Music* consists of concise monographs that help the profession re-imagine how we must prepare 21st Century Musicians. Shifting cultural landscapes, emerging technologies, and a changing profession in-and-out of the academy demand that we re-examine our relationships with audiences, leverage our art to strengthen the communities in which we live and work, equip our students to think and act as artist-entrepreneurs, explore the limitless (and sometimes limiting) role technology plays in the life of a musician, revisit our very assumptions about what artistic excellence means and how personal creativity must be repositioned at the center of this definition, and share best practices and our own stories of successes and failures when leading institutional change.

These short-form books can be either single-authored works, or contributed volumes comprised of 3 or 4 essays on related topics. The books should prove useful for emerging musicians inventing the future they hope to inhabit, faculty rethinking the courses they teach and how they teach them, and administrators guiding curricular innovation and rebranding institutional identity.

Music as Care
Artistry in the Hospital Environment: CMS Emerging Fields in Music
Sarah Hoover

A More Promising Musical Future
Leading Transformational Change in Music Higher Education
Edited by Michael Stepniak

Reimagining Lyric Diction Courses
Leading Change in the Classroom and Beyond
Timothy Cheek

Caring for the Whole Musician
Awareness and Mindfulness
Larry Lee Hensel and Alexander Kahn

Assimilation v. Integration in Music Education
Leading Change toward Greater Equity
Christopher Jenkins

Inclusive Music Histories
Leading Change through Research and Pedagogy
Ayana O. Smith

For more information, please visit: https://www.routledge.com/CMS-Emerging-Fields-in-Music/book-series/CMSEMR

Inclusive Music Histories
Leading Change through Research and Pedagogy

Ayana O. Smith

NEW YORK AND LONDON

First published 2024
by Routledge
605 Third Avenue, New York, NY 10158

and by Routledge
4 Park Square, Milton Park, Abingdon, Oxon, OX14 4RN

Routledge is an imprint of the Taylor & Francis Group, an informa business

© 2024 Ayana O. Smith

The right of Ayana O. Smith to be identified as author of this work has been asserted in accordance with sections 77 and 78 of the Copyright, Designs and Patents Act 1988.

All rights reserved. No part of this book may be reprinted or reproduced or utilised in any form or by any electronic, mechanical, or other means, now known or hereafter invented, including photocopying and recording, or in any information storage or retrieval system, without permission in writing from the publishers.

Trademark notice: Product or corporate names may be trademarks or registered trademarks, and are used only for identification and explanation without intent to infringe.

Library of Congress Cataloging-in-Publication Data
Names: Smith, Ayana O., 1973- author. Title: Inclusive music histories: leading change through research and pedagogy / Ayana O. Smith. Description: [1.] | New York: Routledge, 2023. | Series: CMS emerging fields in music | Includes bibliographical references and index. Identifiers: LCCN 2023024735 (print) | LCCN 2023024736 (ebook) | ISBN 9781032113234 (hardback) | ISBN 9781032113241 (paperback) | ISBN 9781003219385 (ebook) Subjects: LCSH: Music–History and criticism. | Music–Historiography. | Culturally relevant pedagogy. | Curriculum change. Classification: LCC MT1.S544 I53 2023 (print) | LCC MT1. S544 (ebook) | DDC 780.71–dc23/eng/20230710
LC record available at https://lccn.loc.gov/2023024735
LC ebook record available at https://lccn.loc.gov/2023024736

ISBN: 9781032113234 (hbk)
ISBN: 9781032113241 (pbk)
ISBN: 9781003219385 (ebk)

DOI: 10.4324/9781003219385

Typeset in Times New Roman
by Deanta Global Publishing Services, Chennai, India

For my sibling Maya Mesola, with love and gratitude for their support and inspiration

Contents

	Series Editor's Introduction	*viii*
	Acknowledgements	*x*
1	Introduction	1
2	Identity in Historical Narratives	17
3	Representational Tropes in Text, Image, and Music	40
4	Caricature and Character, Appropriation and Authenticity	75
5	Signifying Meaning in African-American Music	92
	Index	*105*

Series Editor's Introduction

Music is embraced throughout every culture without boundaries. Today, an increasingly connected world offers influence and inspiration for opening our imaginations, as technology provides unprecedented access to global audiences. Communities gather around music to mourn collective hardships and celebrate shared moments, and every parent understands that music enhances their child's chances to succeed in life. Yet it has never been more of a struggle for musicians to make a living at their art—at least when following traditional paths.

The College Music Society's *Emerging Fields in Music Series* champions the search for solutions to the most pressing challenges and most influential opportunities presented to the music profession during this time of uncertainty and promise. This series re-examines how we as music professionals can build relationships with audiences, leverage our art to strengthen the communities in which we live and work, equip our students to think and act as artist-entrepreneurs, explore the limitless (and sometimes limiting) role technology plays in the creation and dissemination of music, revisit our very assumptions about what artistic excellence means, and share best practices and our own stories of successes and failures when leading institutional change.

These short-form books are written for emerging musicians busy inventing the future they hope to inherit, faculty rethinking the courses they teach (curriculum) and how they teach them (pedagogy), and administrators rebranding institutional identity and reshaping the student experience.

The world and the profession are changing. And so must we, if we are to carry forward our most beloved traditions of the past and create an audience for our best future.

Leading Change in a time of uncertainty and promise (a collection within the series) offers a comprehensive scaffolding of *why, what, how*, and for *whom* meaningful change is necessary if music schools are to equip students to invent the future they will soon inherit, offer faculty insights for rethinking the courses they teach and how they teach them, and recalibrate administrators' priorities, policies, and procedures as they paint the new landscape of the 21st century music school. The editor's premise for the collection is that institutions of higher learning in music must see their principal role as one that prepares musicians as one-of-a-kind artists-to-the-world, equipped with the requisite knowledge, skills, and understandings to create a lifetime of artistic moments, one after the next.

The collection begins by making the argument for music's "essential" place within the human experience as the foundation of professional and career development. It then offers and examines pillars for change by addressing three fundamental questions facing the profession:

Pillar 1: Whose music matters?
Pillar 2: What might be possible if we were to reposition creativity at the center of all that we do?
Pillar 3: How might individuals and communities, through the work of career musicians and the experience of music, become more joyful, hopeful, connected, and healthy through musical experience?

Each pillar opens with an anchor manuscript that provides a comprehensive approach for imagining change. Subsequent books within each pillar offer specific ways forward.

Finally, three books examine *how* the systems and eco-systems that drive our music schools maintain inequities and obstruct innovation. Examining the academic journeys of students, faculty, and administrators, the authors decode often invisible systems that limit our growth and offer opportunities to realign our words and actions with the goals of fighting for equity, fostering inclusivity, celebrating creativity, and embracing community and the joy inherent within music-making.

In *Inclusive Music Histories: Leading Change through Research and Pedagogy* author Ayana O. Smith challenges us to move beyond increased representation when reimagining pedagogical frameworks if we are to advance musicology as a discipline that is decisively antiracist. While mapping a new approach to teaching music history to Bloom's Taxonomy, Smith unpacks how "othering" signals inferiority, illuminates how "origin myths" eclipses "shadow histories" in traditional historical narratives, and exposes the harm caused by mimicry and mockery of identities and cultures in earlier musical repertories and primary resources.

More importantly, Smith offers flexible scaffolding, case studies, and classroom activities that are driven by inclusivity, informed by Critical Race Theory, and crafted in deep expertise that will guide faculty to choose, structure, and present all aspects of each course taught within a Post-George Floyd music history curriculum.

Mark Rabideau

Acknowledgements

I am grateful for the funding support received from Indiana University, the Racial Justice Research Fund (which helped me develop the Origin Myths and Shadow Histories framework), and from Platform: An Arts and Humanities Research Laboratory (which enabled me to participate in the Global Popular Music Project, and develop material related to the Florence Price and Muddy Waters sections appearing in this book).

Many thanks to colleagues and collaborators, especially Arne Spohr, Devon Nelson, Miguel Arango Calle, and Deanna Pellerano, who worked with me on the Creating Real Change project, and whose feedback helped me to develop the Origin Myths and Shadow Histories material. I am also indebted to colleagues who extended invitations to speak on my Race and Representation projects at conferences and colloquia, enabling me to receive additional feedback through discussion, especially Dana T. Marsh, Emily Francomano, Mauro Calcagno, Joyce Chen, Wendy Heller, and Marysol Quevedo. My colleagues in EMRG (Engaging Music, Race, Gender), including Naomi André, Denise Von Glahn, Tammy Kernodle, Kristen Turner, and others, inspired and encouraged me to think deeply about historiography and the pedagogy of African-American music. With gratitude for Mark Rabideau, who encouraged me to write this book.

1 Introduction

Inclusive Music Histories: Leading Change through Research and Pedagogy addresses the need for serious pedagogical reform in the Western art music tradition. For decades, music scholars have broadened the scope of the repertory and literature taught at the university level, to increase the representation of composers, performers, and authors from diverse backgrounds. These efforts have led to new special topics courses, such as Women in Music, Gender and Sexuality in Music, African-American Music, World Music, Jazz, and Popular Music. Motivated partly by the research-driven New Musicology, multiculturalism, and inclusion—which became prominent in the 1990s—such course topics have enriched the experiences of music students at all levels of the curriculum, while expanding the performance canon that audiences hear in the concert hall.

Yet several significant problems remain. For example, how does the foundational survey course represent or interact with the multiplicity of new approaches to Western art music? How do faculty "cover" an ever-increasing musical canon without losing certain long-standing favorites? Several institutions have developed new methods of presenting the traditional content of the survey class—or have redefined altogether the requirements of the music degree. New questions are surfacing, especially in the wake of racial justice protests of summer 2020 in the U.S. and throughout the world. In this new environment, our priorities have shifted to anti-racism. How can we teach a mostly white musical canon that was created through pathways of elitism and exclusion—often funded by exploitative historical practices, including slavery, colonialism, or other forms of economic and cultural oppression—now, in an ethical way? How can we avoid tokenism when our efforts at inclusion maintain imbalances in ethnic, racial, or gendered representation? How can we prepare our students for a rapidly changing professional world, in which performers and scholars are required to demonstrate competence in more than one style, repertory, or historical field?

Inclusive Music Histories offers a new solution by transforming the role that music history plays in our students' educational and professional lives. I argue that changing the topics that we teach cannot solve our curricular problems—we can only effect real change by reforming *why* and *how* we teach our

DOI: 10.4324/9781003219385-1

2 *Introduction*

repertory. Music history currently serves several purposes in the conservatory and liberal arts classrooms. Students learn to:

1. Recognize a core repertory.
2. Associate specific genres, styles, and forms with major composers, national regions, and chronological eras.
3. Develop critical listening, score study, research, and writing skills.
4. Examine how composers, performance practices, instruments, and musical artifacts intersect with historical, political, philosophical, religious, social, and scientific trends.

I have structured this list so that it maps onto Bloom's well-known pedagogical taxonomy; thus, the first item on my list (core repertory) falls at the base of the pyramid (remember/recognize), while the fourth item (intersectional/historical and critical/analytical) resides near the top (analyze/evaluate). (See Figure 1.1.)

Our current method of curricular reform only addresses the issue of "core repertory" by redefining what is considered "important"—thus operating at the lowest level of Bloom's Taxonomy. This strategy creates a competitive model, whereby—through comparative analysis—we must defend *why* we have chosen these works by these composers, *why* they should be part of the core repertory, and *why* they have value. We take pains to "figure out" *how* and *when* to discuss these works, as if shoehorning them into the curriculum. As a result, we decide what to "cut" to "make space" for this material. Students therefore receive the message, either implicitly or explicitly, that these "othered" topics are either separate from the Western art tradition (and

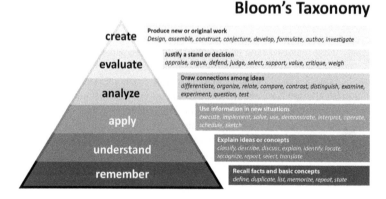

Figure 1.1 **Bloom's Taxonomy.** Courtesy of Vanderbilt University Center for Teaching. https://cft.vanderbilt.edu/guides-sub-pages/blooms-taxonomy/.

therefore elective), or they are an inferior subset of that tradition, because our only motivation for inclusion is to create representation for its own sake.

This "core repertory" model only serves the needs of non-minority students who "need to know" a few things about other traditions, while tokenizing the students of color who are supposed to feel satisfied that someone made a passing reference to their heritage. This message is less apparent when we look at advanced topics courses on individualized subjects such as African-American Music—but these courses are frequently not required; in too many instances they remain isolated from other course offerings. As a result, courses like African-American Music are positioned to create a counter-narrative against the massive, monolithic Western art tradition, instead of intersecting with it. Because a subject cannot be simultaneously "counter to" *and* "foundational to" another subject, this positioning creates an unresolvable paradox, further minimizing African-American music's centrality to the Western art tradition—both in the U.S. and elsewhere. This leaves the "traditional" subjects positioned as "normal," but with gaping holes in musical historical knowledge. Therefore, this model does not fully address the end goal of creating a truly intersectional curriculum, namely, one that articulates in a comprehensive, *truthful* way the critical lenses that help students navigate the world or understand how we ended up where we are today within a global context.

One of the biggest challenges to solve within this curricular project is to address the disconnect between scholarly writing and the pedagogical tools needed by instructors. Therefore, for this book, I have repurposed my original research frameworks toward pedagogical instruction. Although my writing here is geared toward instructional formats, I want to emphasize that the methodologies are inherently scholarly. Until our scholarship shifts toward the directions outlined here, we will not have enough tools to teach a fully inclusive curriculum. Researchers in all areas of music—whether ethnomusicology, musicology, music theory, or performance studies—can advance the project of inclusive music histories by using the tools described here as scholarly methodologies. Only then will we have a complete set of materials available to both instructors and students to expand our musical engagement.

Ethical Representation in the Music History Classroom

The methods offered here address the questions I receive from instructors wishing to diversify their teaching materials. One of the most common questions is, "How do I teach traditional topics and skills while also teaching new or diverse repertoires?" While instructors may feel that teaching new topics or repertory in service of diversity means that they must "give up" the content that feels familiar to them—the "musical canon"—this is not true. Diversity is not anathema to tradition; diversity is part of tradition; we just have been taught not to recognize it. Even traditional subjects, such as early music, can be taught in diverse, ethical ways. We may have to find materials outside of musicology, or creatively combine materials. Even if our goal is not to teach world music or global music histories (which might be the subjects of other courses in your institution's curriculum), we can recognize that Europe was always a diverse place. To find this evidence, simply look—really look—at ancient archeological, artistic, or literary materials. For example, one of the oldest synagogues in Europe was in the ancient Roman port, Ostia Antica.[1] How can we use this knowledge in the music history classroom?

To begin, we must reconcile biases embedded within our current pedagogical practices. When our early music curriculum focuses on Catholic-centered traditions, from the development of chant through motetting practices, we imply that the only musical traditions worth studying are Christian. This traditional history developed because we have relied primarily on sources that originated in the monastic manuscript tradition. Archeology narrates a different story. The archeological history of Ostia Antica tells us that early Rome incorporated a mixture of cultures, languages, and religions. Using images from this ancient site can draw our students into a richer cultural narrative, one that is also more accurate.[2]

To diversify a lecture on ancient music, offer a broad overview of this cultural history. Use this famous synagogue as a focal point, demonstrating how Greek, Jewish, Egyptian, and Roman cultures interacted along the Mediterranean shores. Integrate discussion of newly emerging Christian musical traditions with what we know about the much older Jewish musical traditions.[3] In a subsequent lecture, instead of requiring undergraduate students to memorize every Christian chant genre, or to understand modal theory, focus on how music shapes one Christian and one Jewish ceremony (see Box 1.1). Design an assignment asking students to reflect on how music serves ritual functions in their own lives—whether religious, spiritual, or secular. Require that students use a keyword bank of musical analytical terms when discussing what a ritual performance means, and its relationship to occasion and physical space. Ask students to compare their analysis outcomes with those discussed in class. This structure enables students to learn about two traditions side-by-side, while juxtaposing a more complex "bigger picture" with moments of detailed focus; students also learn traditional analytical skills. Return to music theory later; motets offer opportunities to study the relationship between modes and emerging tonality.

Box 1.1: Lecture Idea—Chant and Liturgy

To update a traditional lecture on Christian plainchant, use maps, timelines, and photographs of religious and musical objects from Ostia Antica to explore how Christian, Jewish, and other communities interacted. Compare the roles for music in early Christian and Jewish holidays, or compare psalmody traditions in both liturgical repertories. (See Boin 2013, J.A. Smith 2010, and Walden, ed. 2015).

Introduction 5

After building this important foundation, add meaningful follow-ups. For later lectures situated in the early modern era, spend a day on Sephardic songs in Spain, and one or more days on Salamone Rossi (1570–1630) and Claudio Monteverdi (1567–1643) in Mantua.[4] Branch out further from each of these additional moments. Demonstrate how some Sephardic songs—especially those narrating Spanish history in the *romancero* tradition—contain important historical themes that resurface in baroque opera. Handel's *Rodrigo, ovvero Vincer se stesso è la maggior vittoria* (Florence, 1707) is an accessible example; students learn baroque forms, instrumentation, and dramatic conventions while comparing how gender, politics, and religion are portrayed in the original Sephardic tales versus in the operatic narrative (see Box 1.2). Return to the text-music analysis skills gained by studying Rossi and Monteverdi in Mantua, when teaching later Venetian opera. Explore Venetian church music involving processions through the city (see Box 1.3)[5] while discussing how those processions interacted with the Jewish ghetto, from the perspectives of architecture, art, and physical space (Box 1.4).[6]

Box 1.2: Analysis Assignment, Research Project—Sephardic Romances and Baroque Opera

Refer to your previous lecture on Sephardic songs by having students review and identify the main narrative elements of the *romancero* "Rey Fernando" (Walden, ed., 2015, 105). Some suggestions: nationalism, identity, kingdoms, family dynamics, battle, peace, promises, treachery, imprisonment, honesty, gender, women as heroes. Then, have students identify how similar historical themes are expressed in excerpts from Handel's opera *Rodrigo, ovvero Vincer se stesso è la maggior vittoria* (1707). How does Handel's opera reinterpret Spanish-origin themes? How do the outcomes differ from the versions expressed in Sephardic song? Who "owns" or "writes" Spanish history?

For advanced graduate students: Assign text and score excerpts from Pollarolo's *La forza della virtù* (1693) or Caldara's *L'Anagilda* (1711) for a comparative approach (A. Smith 2010, 2019). How do the real historical events used as the background to the opera relate to the early eighteenth century, especially regarding religion, gender, politics, and war? How do themes of the Spanish Reconquest and unification, which foreground the expulsions of Moors and Jews from Spain, serve eighteenth-century Italian audiences?

6 *Introduction*

> **Box 1.3: Lecture Idea—Polychoral Style in Mantua and Venice**
>
> On two separate class days, discuss the use of polychoral style in Rossi's *Ha-shirim asher lishlomo,* (*The Songs of Solomon*) (1622), and in Giovanni Gabrieli's "In ecclesiis," from the *Sacrae Symphoniae* (1615). In both instances, situate the texts, the music, and the stylistic features into liturgical practices. For Rossi, discuss how his dual identity as a Jewish musician and as a Mantuan court musician created an intertextuality in text and musical style, but a life that was bifurcated between the Mantuan ghetto and the privileges of court (Jacobson in Walden, ed., 2015).
>
> For Gabrieli's "In ecclesiis," discuss how the liturgical function of the text, for the Festival of the Redeemer, emphasizes the concepts of "space" and "place": *in ecclesiis* (in churches), *in omni loco* (in every place), *in Deo* (in God). Use "space" and "place" to discuss the acoustical properties of performance in St. Mark's Basilica. Use modern maps and images to illustrate the Feast of the Redeemer processional from the Doge's palace to the Church of the Redeemer (Santissimo Redentore) and ending at St. Mark's Basilica. Then, using historical maps and images (Kurtzman 2016, Katz 2017), expand on the concepts of physical, architectural, and cultural space by discussing how Christian processions interacted with the Jewish ghetto in Venice.

> **Box 1.4: Discussion Topic, Reading Assignment—Processions in Venice**
>
> Assign Kurtzman 2016, and Katz 2017 (pp. 86–100) to advanced students. Have students compare the architectural, musical, and visual experiences of early modern Venice for Christian and Jewish communities.

This curricular process creates a "layered pathway." By connecting multiple events across time, we construct a more diverse musical historical narrative, avoiding tokenization. From the historical narrative I provided above, the only figure that consistently appears in textbooks of early music is Salamone Rossi—however, authors mostly discuss his violin music, enabling us to ignore or minimize his identity as a Jewish composer. This approach misinforms students about the presence of Jews, Jewish music, and culture in Europe. Salamone Rossi was not a lonely figure, but a composer whose identity and musical culture had a rich history rooted in Europe, stretching back to ancient Rome; yet even this expanded narrative only scratches the surface.

Create at least three historical connections—each with its own preparatory lecture, assignment, and follow-up throughout the semester—totaling at least nine instructional moments. Whenever we encounter a figure from a marginalized identity in our textbook or in other materials that we use for classroom preparation, locate at least two precedents that can be included in earlier lectures, thus building a layered historical pathway. Expanding beyond the field of musicology, engaging just a few accessible materials from art, archeology, architecture, or literature, and supplementing textbook readings with book chapters on other religious or cultural traditions, we easily create a more inclusive—and ethical—historical narrative.

Throughout this book, you will notice that this process informs all my case studies. Each case study includes usable tools based on my own research methodologies and classroom instruction. The case studies will enrich already available content, making lecture, discussion, and assignment preparation easier. The supplemental boxes provide additional ideas on topics not included in the more detailed case studies. Instructors will find a range of tools designed to enhance their classrooms, while researchers will find interdisciplinary methodologies unlocking new lines of inquiry. This book is not meant to be historically comprehensive; despite its title, it is not meant to include examples regarding every identity. The purpose of this book, rather, is to showcase the techniques, methodologies, and frameworks enabling others to forge their own inclusive scholarship and pedagogy. Using the processes demonstrated here, instructors can design inclusive music histories suitable for their own institutions, while scholars find inspiration to publish materials supporting these efforts.

Case Study 1: A Syllabus on George Frideric Handel (1685–1759)

Combined, the "layered pathway" process and a "shift in thinking" broadens our historical perspectives. The remainder of this book focuses on specific frameworks that close common gaps in our music histories. These are designed for the instructor and the researcher—*not* the student. Students will benefit from the outcomes, but do not need to know or use the methodologies I have designed. (However, these may be helpful for more advanced students, or for graduate students who are training to be classroom leaders.) Thus, this book differs fundamentally from a textbook, or a pedagogical handbook.

The methodological frameworks are equally useful for meta-design—such as constructing a syllabus—as they are for generating detailed course content, such as lectures, assignments, analytical exercises, or discussion prompts. The first case study shows how I updated a traditional syllabus on George Frideric Handel; I combined a "layered pathway" with my methodological frameworks to organize an entire semester plan. In this case study, two frameworks ("Origin Myths and Shadow Histories," Chapter 2; "Mimesis to Mockery,"

8 Introduction

Chapter 3) motivate both structural design and content creation; I reveal how, applied to meta-design levels, the frameworks assist instructors in designing a course with no *apparent* reason for diversity and inclusion.

This case study shows how my approach works within the conservatory environment (where I teach); the academic curriculum must track, at least to a certain extent, the performance canon. With the flexibility of my design, a new feedback loop will exist between performance canon and research canon. When we no longer silo topics related to diversity and inclusion from the canonic works of the Western art music tradition, the expanded academic canon will inspire a more diverse performance canon, through student engagement and our students' future teaching. Approaches that demonstrate performative value through critical analysis rather than composer identity will be more convincing. The extent to which our previous teaching models have tokenized composers from diverse backgrounds has limited the crossover appeal into recital and concert hall repertoires.

At the syllabus design level, my methodological frameworks resulted in the following modules for my graduate composer class on George Frideric Handel (M502: Handel and His World, Spring 2019).

---

1. Instrumental Music and Instrumental Practices; Performance and Sources
2. Baroque Theater; Staging and Gesture; Using and Studying Manuscripts

"Origin Myths and Shadow Histories" Framework:
3. *Giulio Cesare* (1724): Representing History and the "Other;" Egyptology and Intellectual Culture
4. Networks: Handel's Patrons and Contemporaries; Interactions with Colonialism; Blackness in Europe; Biography and Historiography
5. *Messiah* (1741): Musical Semiotics and Religious Disputes; Jews and Jewishness in Europe

"Mimesis to Mockery" Framework:
6. Gender and Sexuality; Exoticism on Stage; Handel's Singers; Handel as Orpheus; Iconography and Caricature

---

In this course, the contrast between "tradition" and "innovation" could not be greater. In a standard historical narrative, Handel typically represents a lineage of Germanic contrapuntal complexity also emblematic of Johann Sebastian Bach (1685–1750), subsequently handed down to Ludwig Van Beethoven (1770–1827), Felix Mendelssohn (1809–1847), and Johannes Brahms (1833–1897). Since Handel perfected his vocal writing in Italy, he also represents the nationalistic narrative of Italian operatic style spreading through northern Europe through

Introduction 9

imitation and emigration. Finally, having completed his career in England, Handel represents aesthetic differences between Italian and English opera.

By shifting the curricular paradigm from "core repertory" to "intersectional/historical" motivations, my syllabus offers an expanded historiography, demonstrating how colonialism, imperialism, religion, politics, and gender influenced composition of certain operas and oratorios. The "Origin Myths and Shadow Histories" framework (Chapter 2) provides counterparts to the "great Germanic composer" narrative, by studying how nationalist themes motivated the earliest editions of Handel's works; the first Handel festivals, conferences, and early scholarship intentionally skewed well-known data to fit political ideology. These topics also lead to classroom conversations about the political manifestations of modern operatic performance, and the meanings embedded in modern scholarship.

The "Origin Myths and Shadow Histories" framework confronts the historiographical narratives that center the classical Greek and Roman traditions as the primary sources of all Western musical materials.[7] By framing parts of Handel's career from an intercultural perspective, students recognize that dramatic representations both reflected and influenced audiences' beliefs about race, gender, and ethnicity—and, that we can interpret those works differently today. Students learn why the classical past served an important function in eighteenth-century literature and opera. How did Handel's operas reflect society while reinforcing societal norms? How can modern performances contend with these issues? These questions help students—whether in conservatories or in liberal arts colleges—imagine new ways of interpreting or performing Handel. And that, in the end, is our educational charge: to equip future scholars and performers with rich histories that inform how they invent the future.

The "Mimesis to Mockery" framework (Chapter 3) teaches students to recognize representational tropes—or stereotypes—embedded in primary sources, and in modern performances. This framework enables students to gain critical analytical skills, through musical, textual, and visual analysis. Whereas the Origin Myths module focuses on historiography, the Mimesis to Mockery module focuses on analytical skill building. Biography and compositional context are centered in both modules. In the latter module, we study representations of Handel and his singers in primary sources, the caricatures and mythological personas that enveloped them, and how their audiences perceived them. We also study the relationship between singers and character types in opera; we investigate how audiences familiar with multiple Handel operas may have made connections between gendered, heroic, and exoticized character types across time.

While research already exists for many of these ideas, they would not rise to the surface as readily if the syllabus were organized around the "core repertory" principle. These ideas only emerge when "intersectional/historical" and "critical/analytical" paradigms are used together, intentionally juxtaposed. The "critical/analytical" paradigm emphasizes musical theoretical skill building to encourage students to develop their own scholarly insights. We study several canonical works (*Giulio Cesare*, *Messiah*, major oratorios, cantatas, and orchestral works), but we also study lesser-known organ and keyboard works. Learning about how Handel's financial, political, and social networks informed his career offers new ways of looking at the eighteenth-century world.

Whereas the "intersectional/historical" paradigm shapes topics and reading assignments, the "critical/analytical" paradigm influences teaching methods. Students gain analytical skills enabling them to differentiate between the rhetorical, structural, linguistic, musical, and visual depictions of gender and ethnicity in Handel's *Giulio Cesare*. (Chapter 2, Case Study 4.) Combined, the "intersectional/historical" design, and the "Origin Myths and Shadow Histories" framework, illustrate the connections between operatic patrons' investment in the slave trade—with representations of Egyptian men as "barbaric," "bloodthirsty," and "lustful," while Egyptian women were associated with "harems," "seduction," and "love." For instructors who want to make additional comparisons to the modern world, it is easy to find ways that the dominant cultures in the U.S. and Europe continue to use similar stereotypes in representations of marginalized groups. We might ask our students to survey recent news, music-related images, or other media for relevant examples to discuss in class.

Case Study 2: A Shift in Thinking—William Grant Still (1895–1978) and the American Music Survey

While the Handel case study engages a topic that seems unrelated to diversity based on the composer's European identity, the second case study demonstrates how to teach a composer who already represents diversity, and therefore, seems to meet the goals of an ethical music history without further intervention. William Grant Still's innovative work, the *Afro-American Symphony* (1935), is now almost universally included in music history survey textbooks, and in advanced classes on American music. Under the current model, this work has "value" as "core repertory" because it was the first symphonic composition by a Black composer to be played by a major orchestra, and because it meets the aesthetic criteria of the Harlem Renaissance by weaving traditionally Black idioms into a classical form. This material is interesting, formative, and worthwhile, but nevertheless tokenizes William Grant Still, since this approach ignores all the other meaningful facets of his contributions to American music while focusing only on those that represent his identity. Too frequently, Black artists and intellectuals are sequestered to speak to the Black experience alone, whereas white artists and intellectuals are invited to speak to the breadth of human experience.

What we need is a shift in thinking—one that prioritizes the fourth pedagogical criteria (*intersectional/historical* and *critical/analytical*) from my list above as reasons for inclusion. Shifting our motivations enables an ethical curriculum. An ethical music history would discuss Still's studies with Edgard

Introduction 11

Varèse (1883–1965), his ultra-modernist techniques *(Darker America*, 1924), his engagement with jazz (*Levee Land*, 1925), his portrayal of Americanist landscapes (*Kaintuck*, 1935), and his musical mysticism (*Seven Traceries*, 1940).[8] Including this full range of perspectives demonstrates that Still was not "just" a member of the Harlem Renaissance movement, but a wide-ranging, quintessentially American composer. Now, the "layered pathway" approach initiates starting points for additional modules using the "Like the Light of Liberty" framework (Chapter 5), while presenting William Grant Still alongside other composers who used similar compositional techniques.

An ethical musical history would question why the scholarly literature on William Grant Still mentions his studies with Varèse, but the scholarly literature on Varèse largely ignores Still. An ethical music history would demonstrate how Still's compositional techniques interacted with compositions by Amy Beach (1867–1944), Charles Ives (1874–1954), Henry Cowell (1897–1965), Duke Ellington (1899–1974), and Ruth Crawford Seeger (1901–1953)—and would investigate whether his contemporaries acknowledged or engaged with his ideas. An ethical music history would discuss Still's own conflicted feelings about how white audiences perceived his music, analyzing the rhetorical tropes used in reviews of his concerts. An ethical music history would question why composers such as Aaron Copland (1900–1990) are centered in American nationalism topics due to his use of folk idioms and imitations of Western cowboy aesthetic (which also reinforces the false idea of an "all-white West"), but African-American music is rarely discussed under units on "nationalism" (except to the extent that composers, such as Antonín Dvořák [1841–1904], encouraged the use of Native American and Negro folk tunes to create a supposedly "authentic" sound). An ethical music history would juxtapose various critiques against jazz with arguments defining Black vernacular as the only original American sound. An ethical music history would then study how jazz influenced European music, using these examples not as passing references but engaging deep analysis of harmonic, structural, and rhythmic borrowings.

An ethical music history would explain the cultural references to dance (for example, fox trot, turkey trot, cakewalk, juba) in concert music—but would also juxtapose these against original materials in African-American folk musics so that students learn to differentiate between caricature and character. An ethical music history would contextualize European musical references to such dance gestures with minstrelsy exported via the Paris Expositions (1889, 1900)—and from there into musical theater and film. (Chapters 3, 4.) An ethical music history would return to traditionally marginalized figures multiple times in different contexts to flesh out their full humanity, using the "layered pathway" process, so they need not remain footnotes in a whitewashed narrative. An ethical music history still includes major topics central to music historiography, but represents a fuller, more *truthful* account. An ethical music history offers richer intellectual engagement precisely because it centers the perspectives of those who were, and continue to be, marginalized. When we fully explicate the intellectual histories of marginalized musics—meeting the educational needs of marginalized students—everyone benefits.

The above paragraphs demonstrate the vibrancy that emerges when we do full justice to marginalized composers. By centering William Grant Still, I created a series of intersectional topics covering a historical swath from the 1890s to the 1940s, encompassing genres from the vernacular to jazz, concert music, and film, traveling through major metropolitan areas in the U.S. and Europe, engaging textual and musical analysis while investigating racial, gendered, rhetorical, cultural, national, and commercial dynamics. I also want to emphasize that "centering" does not mean "dominating." I am not substituting a Black historical frame for a white historical frame. I am simply starting from the reality that tokenization is harmful; I am undoing that harm by treating Black and other marginalized composers as fully as their white, predominantly male, counterparts. In doing so, this curriculum reveals how race and gender become imprinted in culture, discourse, and historiography. This last point is crucial, because *not* studying these prejudicial dynamics as a form of intellectual history allows us to repeat them. *Not* teaching these ideas is more dangerous than being more inclusive. *Not* teaching these ideas allows a biased, incomplete version of history to continue supporting the notion that white cultural products are inherently superior, and that Black, female, and other marginalized composers were excluded because of *their inability* instead of by *our intentional choice*.

My approach is flexible, highly adaptable, and can transform any subject that we currently teach, whether chronologically or topically organized. Even medieval chant, or Renaissance motets can be taught in this way. (Chapter 2, Case Study 3.) The shift in thinking occurs such that we open our eyes and ears to new combinations of musical materials instead of centering solely the white, Christian perspective. After all, Western Europe itself always encompassed much more diversity than our music history pedagogy suggests. Why should we continue to silence these voices?

The shift in thinking begins with the question: what is the *critical/analytical* or *intersectional/historical* reason for teaching this work? A simple shift from *repertory* to *function* enables us to stop valuing certain musical works simply because we have always valued them—a circular logic that re-inscribes whiteness—as the primary limiting factor for perceived "excellence." For example, medieval chant repertory teaches comprehension of modal sonorities. Instead, design a class about different ways of organizing melody. Or, medieval chant repertory teaches how music shapes and reflects liturgy. Instead, consider Christian, Jewish, Muslim, or other religious musical practices. Or, expand to music and ritual; juxtapose secular and sacred ritual spaces, or medieval and modern eras. Together, the four frameworks create comprehensive, intersectional diversity. For any era, composer, topic, genre, style, or theoretical technique there is an appropriate methodological framework.

Introduction 13

My method works because core principles govern how to choose, structure, and present all aspects of each course. By adhering to these core principles, anyone can duplicate the intellectually satisfying, historically *truthful*, and presently ethical results I have been able to provide to my students in the classroom. The principles and frameworks are applicable in any class, regardless of subject matter, chronological era, or geographical region. This is a crucial aspect of *Inclusive Music Histories*, since it allows maximum flexibility while supporting undergraduate and graduate level curricular reform. The principles and methodologies are appropriate for liberal arts institutions, conservatories, or other performance-based programs alike, regardless of instructional level.

Using the frameworks flexibly, implementing them at different stages of course design, instructors can revise everything from repertory, video and audio recordings, assigned readings, research papers, and in-class discussion activities—or make smaller modifications. The frameworks can inform individual lectures, modules, or the entire course; if there is continuity, and engagement across at least three stages, instructors will avoid harmful tokenizing. Even "traditional" course subjects can become more inclusive by using one or more of the methodological frameworks I have created.

Each chapter provides guiding principles, describing the pedagogical shift from "core repertory" to the "critical/analytical" and "intersectional/historical" approaches to music history, assisting instructors with implementing the overall course goals. Each chapter introduces one framework; historical background, definition of the framework and why it is necessary, and suggestions for implementation are the central focus. Each chapter includes one or more case studies, with instructional boxes providing direct models for syllabus, module, lecture, class activity, discussion prompts, and listening exercises on related topics. Because the case studies and instructional boxes are derived from my own teaching and scholarly activity, they are mostly limited to the subjects I study most: early music, opera, women composers, and African-American music, with one exception—music by Indigenous American composer Brent Michael Davids. (Chapter 4, Case Study 10.) Combining the shifts in thinking, the layered pathways, the frameworks, the case studies, and the instructional boxes, instructors can adopt new inventive practices, layer these to create longer units, and expand multiplicatively to include music by composers of all backgrounds. In this endeavor, we are only limited by our creativity.

Notes

1 Douglas Boin, *Ostia in Late Antiquity* (New York: Cambridge University Press, 2013), 119–124, 155–164, 175–176. https://doi.org/10.1017/CBO9781139161909.
2 For images that may be used in the classroom, see: "Ostia Antica, Detail of the remains of the synagogue, depicting menorah relief," https://library.artstor.org/asset/SS36428_36428_31323161.

14 *Introduction*

3 John Arthur Smith, *Music in Ancient Judaism and Early Christianity* (Burlington, VT: Ashgate, 2010).
4 See Susana Weich-Shahak, "The Traditional Performance of Sephardic Songs, Then and Now," (104–18) and Joshua R. Jacobson, "Art Music and Jewish Culture Before the Jewish Enlightenment," (143–55) in Joshua S. Walden, ed., *The Cambridge Companion to Jewish Music*, Cambridge Companions to Music (Cambridge, United Kingdom: Cambridge University Press, 2015); https://doi.org/10.1017/CCO9781139151214.
5 For an image of the Procession of the Redeemer that can be used in class, see: Giovanni Battista Brustolon, after Antonio Canaletto. "Populi frequentia nocturna," from *Prospectum Aedium* (Venice, 1763). Etching: 329mm x 445mm. British Museum, item number 1868,0208.85. https://www.britishmuseum.org/collection/object/P_1868-0208-85.
6 Dana E. Katz, *The Jewish Ghetto and the Visual Imagination of Early Modern Venice* (New York, NY: Cambridge University Press, 2017).
7 Ayana O. Smith, "Editorial," *Eighteenth Century Music* 18, no. 2 (September 2021): 245–51, https://doi.org/10.1017/S1478570621000105.
8 Horace J. Maxile, Jr., "Extensions to the Pedagogical Canon: Expanding Perspectives on William Grant Still and the Teaching Applications as Realized in the *Seven Traceries*," *College Music Symposium* 55 (2015), https://www.jstor.org/stable/26574396.

Annotated Bibliography

Jewish Music and Culture in Ancient and Early Modern Europe

Boin, Douglas. *Ostia in Late Antiquity*. New York: Cambridge University Press, 2013. https://doi.org/10.1017/CBO9781139161909.

Traces the history of the ancient Roman sea port and its archeological monuments; discusses cultural transformations in late antiquity, as Roman, Christian, Egyptian, Mithraic, and Jewish religious groups interacted. Use the maps, timelines, and photographs of religious and musical objects included in this volume to illustrate how religious communities developed alongside each other. (Box 1.1.)

Katz, Dana E. *The Jewish Ghetto and the Visual Imagination of Early Modern Venice*. New York, NY: Cambridge University Press, 2017.

Analyzes the early modern Jewish ghetto from the perspectives of architectural and urban space. Sections on St. Mark's Square (Piazza San Marco) complement lectures on Venetian church music (pp. 24–25, 49–52) and liturgical processions through the city (pp. 86–89)—especially for the Feast of the Redeemer, the liturgical occasion for Gabrieli's "In ecclesiis." Katz discusses the segmentation of other identity groups based on ethnicity, religion (such as Muslims, Lutherans), or gender in Venice. The section on cloistering (pp. 58–66) includes quotations from primary texts and references to early modern art that would complement a lecture on nuns' music-making, or on the separation of women from public life in general (gendered instruments, educational manuals, *concerto delle donne*, etc.). Includes many historical maps and modern photos. (Box 1.3, 1.4, 1.5.)

Introduction 15

Box 1.5: Lecture Idea, Discussion Topic—Cloistering and Women Composers

Discuss the lives of women composers from the perspectives of public and private engagement in the early modern era. Under what circumstances were women allowed to perform in public, and to what extent did their audiences have access to seeing their physical presence? Examples: nuns composing, singing, and playing instruments in cloistered environments, liturgical dramas, the *intermedii* in Florence, the concerto *delle donne*, domestic music lessons and performances, the *Ospedali* in Venice, opera in court and public theaters. How might we compare the secluded lives of women to the religious and ethnic segmentation discussed in Katz 2017?

Walden, Joshua S., ed. *The Cambridge Companion to Jewish Music.* Cambridge Companions to Music. Cambridge: Cambridge University Press, 2015. https://doi.org/10.1017/CCO9781139151214.

A comprehensive, must-read source on the meanings, rituals, contexts, and social aspects of Jewish music from antiquity to the present, with specialized essays on ontologies, diaspora, institutions, liturgy, folk musics, art music, theater, and cinema. Chapter 6 ("Jewish Liturgical Music," pp. 84–103) by Mark Kligman includes a comparative discussion of religious music in ancient and early modern Europe, including notation, cantillation, psalmody, modes, and liturgy (see esp. pp. 87–92). Chapter 7 ("The Traditional Performance of Sephardic Songs," pp. 104–18) by Susana Weich-Shakak discusses this repertory's cultural, musical, and literary meanings, including its modern performance traditions in North Africa and the Eastern Mediterranean. (Box 1.1, 1.2.)

Smith, John Arthur. *Music in Ancient Judaism and Early Christianity.* Burlington, VT: Ashgate, 2010.

Although this book has several limitations (among them, transliteration issues rendering *shofar* as "sopar" and *nevel* as "nebel"), it is a comprehensive source on music in Biblical sources. The final section compares Jewish and early Christian musical practices, and as readers will discover, the theoretical and practical systems diverged greatly. Useful for lecture-building components if needing a broad overview, especially in conjunction with Chapter 6 from Walden, ed. 2015 . (Box 1.1.)

Processions in Venetian Civic and Religious Practice

Kurtzman, Jeffrey G. "Civic Identity and Civic Glue: Venetian Processions and Ceremonies of the Sixteenth and Seventeenth Centuries." *Yale Journal of Music & Religion* 2, no. 2 (2016). https://doi.org/10.17132/2377-231X.1052.

A suitable reading assignment for graduate students and advanced undergraduates, this article provides an overview of the civic and religious functions of processions in Venice, including for the Feast of the Redeemer. Includes illustrations that are useful for lecture building. Instructors may wish to contrast the notions of "unity" described here, with "segmentation" as described in Katz. (Box 1.3, 1.4.)

Origin Myths and Shadow Histories

Smith, Ayana O. "Editorial." *Eighteenth Century Music* 18, no. 2 (September 2021): 245–51. https://doi.org/10.1017/S1478570621000105.

Explains the philosophical background for the "Origin Myths and Shadow Histories" framework in brief, clear language, while situating the need for such an approach in operatic studies and in professional institutions. (See also: Chapter 2.)

Baroque Opera

Smith, Ayana O. "Deceiving the Eye: Mirror, Statue, and Stone in Carlo Francesco Pollarolo's *La Forza Della Virtù*." In *Dreaming with Open Eyes: Opera, Aesthetics, and Perception in Arcadian Rome*, 1st ed., 173–209. University of California Press, 2018. https://doi.org/10.2307/j.ctv9zch1q.12.

Although the focus of this chapter is how the Arcadian Academy in Rome used visual culture to define their own literary aesthetics, graduate students could use the textual and musical analysis to discuss the broader implications of performing Spanish history in Italy. (Box 1.2.)

———. "The Mock Heroic, An Intruder in Arcadia: Girolamo Gigli, Antonio Caldara and *L'Anagilda* (Rome, 1711)." *Eighteenth Century Music* 7, no. 1 (March 2010): 35–62. https://doi.org/10.1017/S1478570609990443.

This article discusses how Gigli and Caldara promoted Arcadian Academy operatic reforms; graduate students could use the textual and musical examples to examine how Spanish-themed representations of empire, gender, and ethnicity (especially comic references to Moors) shaped Italian political identities. (Box 1.2.)

William Grant Still

Maxile, Jr., Horace J. "Extensions to the Pedagogical Canon: Expanding Perspectives on William Grant Still and the Teaching Applications as Realized in the *Seven Traceries*." *College Music Symposium* 55 (2015). https://www.jstor.org/stable/26574396.

Maxile reviews recent scholarship on Still, identifies unexplored areas, and provides a detailed theoretical analysis of excerpts from *Seven Traceries* (1940). Use this article for lectures on ultramodern style, to connect historical and theoretical approaches in the classroom, and expand beyond the composer's African-American idioms.

Von Glahn, Denise. *The Sounds of Place: Music and the American Cultural Landscape*. Boston: Northeastern University Press, 2003.

Chapters 3 and 4 compare musical depictions of urban and rural landscapes in music by Still and Duke Ellington. Instructors may want to assign Still's *Kaintuck* (1935) and *Lenox Avenue* (1937), followed by Ellington's *Harlem Air Shaft* (1940) and *Harlem* (1951), to discuss the various representational means used by the two composers. Instructors may also wish to discuss how we define "art music," "symphony," and "jazz." (See also: Chapter 5, Case Study 11.) Discussion topic: How can we reorient our definitions of American musical nationalism around African-American and Indigenous experiences of place and landscape? (See also: Chapter 4, Case Studies 9 and 10, Box 4.3.)

2 Identity in Historical Narratives

Chapter 2 identifies "origin myths" as a problematic feature of the narrative history of Western art music.[1] Although the term "origin myths" can have several connotations—such as mythical creation stories or narratives of religious, political, or national origins—here I define "origin myths" as the collective narrative strategies used to position "Western civilization" as the origination of music in many textbooks. Our starting places for telling stories represent intentionality;[2] when we begin our history surveys with ancient Greek music and medieval Latin chants, we are centering the narratives of Renaissance humanists who claimed those as their intellectual heritage. By doing so, we treat all music history after the Renaissance as being connected to or growing out of that starting point, and we therefore position other musical traditions as lacking a relevant genealogy in Western art music. Thus, the cultural traditions of underrepresented minorities are left as "hanging chads" unable to be fully integrated or interpreted.

Origin myths can also function as identity-based stereotypes that garner wide-spread belief—for example, fictionalized narratives embedded in European music that portray "othered" identities in character music or in opera. For each origin myth there exists a corresponding, authentic, "shadow history" waiting to be told in fuller detail. Understanding origin myths in conjunction with shadow histories provides a mechanism for exploring complex representational strategies about identity, and for learning more about the lived experiences of past and present minoritized cultures in global and American contexts.[3]

Applying the "shift in thinking" defined in Chapter 1 to the Origin Myths and Shadow Histories framework enables greater intentionality regarding inclusivity; juxtaposing diverse materials from similar vantage points—such as uses of melody in various ritual contexts or showing how motets and mash-ups involve the same intellectual and musical procedures (see Case Study 3)—offers a more comprehensive approach to music history and historiography. To "shift our thinking" we can focus less on the traditional, chronologically unfolding, linear, and genealogical approach, and emphasize the musical techniques that creators used to add layered meanings to pre-existing materials.

DOI: 10.4324/9781003219385-2

18 *Identity in Historical Narratives*

The case studies in this chapter (Case Studies 3, 4, and 5)—"Motets and Mashups," "George Frideric Handel's *Giulio Cesare*," and "Scott Joplin's *Treemonisha*"—all help scholars, instructors, and students think carefully about origin myths (whether of history or of identity) while highlighting shadow histories. Case Study 3, "Motets and Mashups," provides a more accessible introduction to motetting practices by using mashups as a modern corollary, while centering the layering of text and music to create new meanings as a cultural and intellectual practice that also occurs within the African-American community. In other words, complexity is not a quality that only exists in European music. The compositional techniques behind motetting did not give way to even more complex styles as tonality developed (a linear, or genealogical way of viewing history); rather, the same underlying techniques exist today using new technologies.

Case Study 4, "George Frideric Handel's *Giulio Cesare*," explores how baroque opera conveys "othered" voices and identities as morally inferior but culturally enticing. This origin myth consolidates European identity as a common inheritance of the ancient Greek and Roman world, and marks non-European identities as "exotic" (or inferior); we often do not recognize these origin myths as problematic, because we are so influenced by the narratives of "Western civilization" and nineteenth-century exoticisms. Case Study 5, "Scott Joplin's *Treemonisha*," brings an early African-American opera to the center, teaches about the folk musics that Scott Joplin (1868–1917) referenced, and explores the prevalent cultural issues depicted in the opera that precipitated the emerging Harlem Renaissance.

Case Study 3: Motets and Mashups—Josquin Des Prez and Danger Mouse

This case study offers an alternative lesson plan on motets in the Western tradition—a subject that frequently follows medieval chant, early polyphony, or secular *formes fixes*. Using the strategies of shifting our thinking and creating layered pathways as described in Chapter 1, Case Study 3 broadens the tools instructors will have at their disposal to modify the traditional opening units on medieval and Renaissance music in a survey class.

To begin the process, we must consider what our educational goals are with teaching motet repertory, which can serve multiple purposes in our curriculum. Studying motets enhances students' understanding of Catholic liturgy; demonstrates how composers interacted with pre-existing materials such as plainchant or popular song as musical structures for elaboration; illustrates the development of Western modal and tonal theory—through counterpoint, cadential formulas, sol-fa and hexachords—and teaches the principles of rhythmic and metrical organization (as in imitation, canon, or isorhythm, etc.). (See Box 2.1, 2.2, Figure 2.1.) To create layered pathways with materials developed earlier, we can build the same skills by teaching repertories from other religious backgrounds, or by using comparative approaches.

Box 2.1: Lecture Idea—Music Theory, Modes, and Early Music

If you have not discussed theoretical concepts (such as modes) in medieval music, now is a good time to introduce these ideas. It often helps students to understand these concepts from the perspective of how they are related to modern systems of pitch and rhythm. For example, most students know modern concepts of solfege with movable *do*; thus, sol-fa of the medieval and Renaissance eras is not a stretch. With this foundation, students can understand how the hexachordal systems developed into modern scales. The first few chapters of Fitch's *Renaissance Polyphony* offer examples that are useful for lecture building (See Fitch 2020). Since the writing is clear and concise, some excerpts of this book could be used for reading assignments.

Box 2.2: Classroom Activity—Hexachords and Sol-fa

Have students learn the Guidonian hand to practice using and understanding hexachordal theory. Using the secular melody *L'homme armé*, have students "sign" one or more phrases. For students who have had at least one semester of music theory, deepen this exercise by having them compose cadences for one or two phrases of the tune. Fitch, Chapter 4 has all the needed materials for these two exercises.

To go deeper into shifting our thinking, however, we also need to deconstruct the origin myth and shadow history dynamic that exists in our traditional narrative. Because motets have many complex musical features, they involve layered meanings that bring intellectual complexity to the new theoretical challenges of this repertory. Because the tradition is embedded in elite musical patronage structures that skew our focus toward male centric realms of compositional activity, it is easy for students to imagine that the motet tradition in the Catholic Church is the locus and height of all musical creativity up until this point in a chronological sequence. To counteract this impression, it is important to illustrate the musical practices overshadowed by motets in our traditional narratives. One way to do this, while remaining focused on the early modern period, is to include motets—or other complex compositional styles—composed by women. (See Box 2.3.) In this case, instructors could discuss the forces

20 *Identity in Historical Narratives*

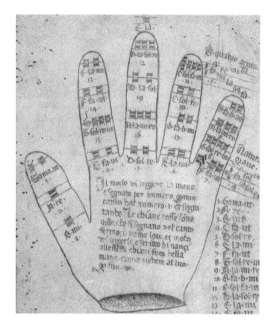

Figure 2.1 **Guidonian Hand.** From a manuscript from Mantua, last quarter of 15th century (Bodleian Library, Oxford University MS Canon. Liturg. 216. f.168 recto.). Courtesy of *Wikimedia Commons, the free media repository*. https://commons.wikimedia.org/w/index.php?title=File:Guidonian_hand .jpg&oldid=297886730 (accessed May 7, 2022).

that prevented women from being as prominently involved (or as prominently researched) in professional musical activities during this era—such as education, cloistering, patronage and funding, and official prohibitions targeted toward convents.

**Box 2.3: Classroom Activity and Assignment—
Hexachordal Analysis, Women in the Renaissance**

To use hexachordal theory as an analytical tool—while incorporating music by women composers—have students "translate" the opening phrases of Maddalena Casulana's (fl. 1566-83) "Morte che voi" into sol-fa syllables. For students comfortable singing together, have them sing the lines with sol-fa. When does Casulana shift from one hexachord to another? Are there potential textual meanings that are brought

> out when she makes these shifts? This activity can be done in small groups in class, so that the instructor can help students with the process. To follow up, have students read Peter Schubert's essay "'Per lei pos' in oblio' from *Cinta di fior* (1570)" in Parsons and Ravenscroft, eds. *Analytical Essays on Music by Women Composers vol. 1* to gain more experience with analysis and with interpreting the analytical techniques used by music scholars. Make sure to discuss the social position and educational opportunities afforded to women in churches, convents, and in secular society, and their participation in the polyphonic tradition.

In this case study, I illustrate just one of the fundamental aspects of motets and their meanings—the layering of musical and textual ideas to create a new commentary. By demonstrating how compositional layering works in modern popular music, we bring several advantages to the classroom. First, we show that the impulse to create musical commentary using language, quotation, and manipulation of sounds is alive and well today, and is an enduring musical instinct. Most importantly, however, we show that complexity is not something that develops from one starting point (the Renaissance) and continues to grow in a linear fashion over time. Rather, every era has its own musical complexity and its own methods for creating hidden symbolisms requiring either insider knowledge or interpretive strategies to unravel. (See Chapter 5 on signifying in African-American music.) Second, we cannot assume that our students can easily enter or participate in the musical materials of the Renaissance without prior knowledge—and we cannot assume prior knowledge of this repertory. Most students, even in a conservatory setting, will have little to no performance experience with medieval or Renaissance vocal music, and they also may not have much background in listening to this music at concerts, in religious venues, or at home.

Introducing motet practices from the perspective of modern popular music that demonstrates similar layering and commenting strategies can enliven the classroom, open students' perceptions, and stimulate their ability to relate to the motet genre. Instructors might explore the various ways that composers have quoted, used, or alluded to pre-existing music through processes that are comparable to counterpoint. This strategy can be used in one or two classes—or could form a chronological unit. For the latter, instructors could use the overview of compositional processes from Adams, "What Did Danger Mouse Do?"[4] to showcase a variety of genres, styles, and cultural backgrounds. At the end of the unit, students could write a short analytical essay comparing the techniques used in two works from different time periods.

By exploring how Renaissance popular songs can be "configurable"—like modern mashups—into different musical contexts through the tools (technology) of counterpoint, students can study how such juxtapositions result in new meanings. Chapter 9 ("Understanding Musical Borrowing") of Fitch, *Renaissance Polyphony* includes several examples that can be used in class or assigned as homework;[5] students can be asked to study the original secular material and compare it to the resulting motet or mass to think about how the textual meaning is changed. In comparison, students could explore some of the original materials used to create Danger Mouse's *The Grey Album* (2004), namely, Jay-Z's *The Black Album* (2003) and The Beatles' *The White Album* (1968).

For advanced students, instructors may wish to explore additional topics. Studying Renaissance motets based on popular songs can involve evaluating textual themes related to gender, identity, or politics in early modern and modern contexts, and thinking about how many representational tropes or stereotypes may still exist today. To extend the musical analogy to the modern era, students can compare the use of popular musics in religious settings or vice versa (i.e., gospel-infused popular musics, or rock-influenced religious musics). Scholarship that revises Josquin des Prez's (c. 1450–1521) (or another composer's) biography can inspire discussions of authorship and authority; how do our perceptions of a composer shift when we learn new details about a composer's location, colleagues, and the music they performed or had access to?

Performance students may be particularly interested in considering how Josquin's role as a singer at the Sistine Chapel influenced his musical style, and the extent to which counterpoint could arise from performative competition, imitation, or improvisation; comparisons could be made regarding how Danger Mouse uses similar strategies to create performative utterances through mashups. This activity could lead to thinking of the Sistine Chapel library as a repository that inspired composition in the same way that popular music albums are repositories of cultural and musical knowledge.[6]

Using the approaches suggested here, the resulting classes juxtapose early and modern materials, integrate Black creativity firmly into the intellectual history of music, and expose a shadow history—namely, that Black popular music artists use technological means to engage in literary and musical practices of troping and signifying (see Chapter 5), effecting forms of cultural heritage building and social protest (see esp. Danger Mouse, "99 Problems"), while contributing to intellectual history.

Before we introduce repertory like Danger Mouse's "99 Problems" (and some older repertory), we need to be intentional about how we plan to use language in class—especially when referring to ethnic identities, and when studying musics that incorporate slang that could be insensitive or even harmful. I advocate the position that we should never use derogatory language in class, even if we are simply quoting language that others have used. Although our students (and we ourselves) are accustomed to hearing and using slang terms in certain contexts, I have a firm belief that we should only use respectful language in the classroom so that we maintain a professional environment, and one that is accessible for all students.

Other professors and ethicists may have different fault lines and may think it is acceptable to quote any offensive language where it was used historically. However, I believe that—considering how hard it is to even read derogatory words—we need to keep them at a distance. Voicing them gives them too much power, and any circumstance in which students are felt to be demeaned is one where learning cannot happen.

Since there have been several incidents that have gained media attention, where students have made formal complaints around the use of the word "negro," I feel it is important to point out, that although this term should not be used to refer to people today, at the time that it was being used as an ethnic category it was not an offensive term but the equivalent of our modern-day terms "African American" or "Black." In fact, it was the term preferred by Black communities in the U.S. Therefore, when referring to historical sources that use this term in titles or in texts that we wish to quote, there should be no discomfort or outrage.

It is helpful for instructors to discuss this topic in advance, by first setting out clear policies regarding respectful dialogue in the syllabus, explicitly defining and reviewing them on the first day of the semester, and then reiterating these principles at the beginning of relevant class discussion days. If your institution has policies regarding microaggressions or hate speech, link or quote those in your syllabus and require your students to read them. Ensure that they understand not only the policies but how these policies mitigate harm. Consider a follow-up "syllabus quiz," which can cover all aspects of your class policies.

Case Study 4: George Frideric Handel's *Giulio Cesare* (1724)—Egypt in the European Imagination; Cleopatra, Past and Present

In recent decades, musicology has made advancements in analyzing how identity is represented in baroque music (and in early music at large). By using tools such as gender criticism and postcolonial studies, scholars have discovered persistent, revealing patterns in how women, gender, sexuality, voice, and ethnicity (especially regarding Native Americans) were represented in baroque opera; scholars have also raised concerns that should be considered in modern performances of this repertory. Musicological scholarship, however, has not entirely figured out how to grapple with the concepts of "exoticism" in this genre. Part of the problem is, that "exoticism" may not even be the right term to use.[7] Since our modern day understanding of exoticism has been so heavily influenced by the nineteenth-century manifestation of this concept (think *Carmen* or *Aida* for example)—and by Edward Said's definition of "orientalism"—we often fail to recognize the similar power dynamics of race, ethnicity, and gender when they show up in pre-nineteenth-century productions. The language in baroque operatic texts was written for audiences that viewed ethnicities according to different paradigms compared to our modern

24 *Identity in Historical Narratives*

definitions; therefore, I believe we need to develop more comprehensive tools for recognizing social hierarchies in this repertory. As a result of differing cultural priorities and experiences, the baroque operatic language focuses more on concepts drawn from classical literature regarding power, ethics, virtue, and behavior rather than the physical details that we, today, associate with race, skin color, or so-called foreignness.

This does not mean, however, that "race" as a concept is not applicable to baroque opera. Racial representation existed long before the word "race" was used as a categorical term in the modern sense. Instead of the word "race," baroque operatic sources use the ethnic terms "Moors," "Turks," "Jews," "Asians," and "Savages." "Moors" referred to almost anyone with dark skin, from a range of places including North and Northwest Africa, Spain, or of Arab heritage. "Turks" referred mostly to those from the Ottoman Empire, including Central Asia, the Middle East, North Africa, and Southeast Europe, or anyone of Islamic belief or Arabic language group—and here you can start to see both differentiation from and overlap with the "Moors." The term "Jews," much like today, was both a religious and ethnic identity, often having a wide geographical overlap with Moors and Turks, but also of course residing within Europe. The term "Asians" could refer to those from ancient Asia Minor (which later became Byzantium and part of the Ottoman Empire), or, in terms contemporary to the baroque era, "Asian" could mean East Asia, the Indian subcontinent or Southeast Asia, and the "East Indies" (remembering that the many European "East India" trading companies also trafficked African slaves to Europe and the Americas). Although many major countries that we now consider "Asian" are not mentioned in baroque opera, China is named as a specific place. The term "Savages" can mean Native Americans, Africans, Indigenous people from modern day Latin or South America, or anyone not considered part of European "civilization."

These designations—which refer just as much to skin color as to geographic, ethnic, national, and religious distinctions—tell us that race as the concept that we recognize today was alive and well in the seventeenth century. If the concept of racial difference did not exist, the Atlantic slave trade could not have existed. And yet it did exist, and endured for hundreds of years, and was codified in laws, philosophy, emerging anthropological and sociological disciplines, and even science—all of which continued to create a vicious cycle by using "evidence" to justify discrimination, segregation, and denial of civil rights, all the way up until the end of the middle third of the twentieth century (in the U.S.), and enabled colonial practices up through the Second World War (in Europe). In contrast, the early modern Mediterranean slave trade (forced labor for political, military, and religious opponents or captors from different nationalities) was not based on race, but on religious difference.[8]

It is important for instructors to be educated on these differences, since a common response from those wishing to minimize the horrors of race-based slavery and discrimination is, "What about the Mediterranean slave trade?"

or, "What about ancient slavery?" A common form of resisting the historical reality that race-based thinking existed—and is relevant to seventeenth-century Europe and its cultural productions—is, "'race' as a modern concept did not exist." These are mental gymnastics that belie the shadow histories—the truths we can discover in primary sources—and continue to propagate origin myths. The first two questions represent a form of "whataboutism" that seeks to compare apples and oranges to claim that oranges are not fruit. The final question is based on a linguistic turn; language changes over time, but that does not mean that whole categories of thought—which are evidenced in historical realities—did not exist.

The Mediterranean slave trade began dwindling towards the end of the second half of the seventeenth century and had ended by the middle of the eighteenth century, when the economic, political, and religious practices that drove it ceased to exist—and began to be considered unethical—but the race-based slavery of Black Africans continued for more than another one hundred years. These historical patterns tell us very clearly that race, Blackness, and ethnic difference were at the center of European political, economic, social, and cultural ideologies and were overtly expressed in the early modern and baroque eras. I also want to make clear that although Jewish and Muslim identities were racialized during the early modern period, and marked as "others," they suffered different types of oppression in Europe even though they were not part of the Atlantic slave trade (except for those with sub-Saharan African origins). Therefore, as music historians and scholars, we must reconcile ourselves to the idea that as we interact with literary, musical, and philosophical sources from this era, we are witnessing racialized doctrines developing right in front of our very eyes—as we continue to study those materials today.

For these reasons, our current definitions of the term "exoticism" do not fully encompass the historical realities of the ethnic and religious differences portrayed in baroque opera. Since our mindsets are still beholden to nineteenth-century notions of exoticism, and since we have not fully investigated the extent to which racialized thinking shows up in the primary sources related to baroque opera, we have not been prepared to recognize race and its representation in representative and dramatic genres. Our current focus on exoticism as a category of difference causes us to exclude a significant amount of musical repertory from our scholarship and pedagogy about early modern and baroque identity, and therefore to essentially deny that representations of race are relevant. Nevertheless, baroque opera clearly and frequently defines characters as "others," portraying identity-based hierarchies with clearly negative political and social consequences.

To counteract the origin myth that race is not relevant to baroque opera (and the resulting misconceptions about the representation of identity in this repertory), we need to investigate the interactions with "othered" identities from interdisciplinary primary sources, including art, history, geography, and literature. Only then will we be able to recognize the role that representation of race, ethnicity, nationality, and gender (or other politicized identities) plays in dramatic productions.

The character of Cleopatra (Cleopatra VII Philopator, Queen of Egypt) in George Frideric Handel's *Giulio Cesare* is an interesting case study, since we can compare ancient and early modern texts and images to modern productions. Although ancient and early modern representations of Cleopatra are not often racially marked (there is debate about this in scholarship on William Shakespeare's *Antony and Cleopatra*, and there is contrary evidence in Spanish plays of the period), they are marked by gendered stereotypes that nevertheless portray her as "different" or "dangerous." Modern video productions of the opera either portray Cleopatra as an "exoticized" character—or, as one that meets ancient, classical, Roman ideals. While comparing text, image, and music across different countries and time periods, and engaging with materials from modern and popular culture, students can interrogate their own expectations, understandings, awareness, and beliefs about race, gender, and ethnicity—while critiquing the rhetorical and cultural possessiveness over this powerful historical figure.

The benefit of studying Cleopatra from this perspective, is that we can explore how ideas about race and ethnicity have changed over time, and we can encourage students to think about how we should portray ethnic difference on stage in more ethical ways. We can explore how Afro-futuristic portrayals of Cleopatra (seeking to create Black role models) or race-blind casting approaches may have fueled complaints of "blackwashing" (objections to casting Black actors and actresses to portray powerful historical figures), hiding behind the guise of "historicism" as a pretext for racism. Given this matrix, students can be encouraged to consider the role of science in its numerous DNA analyses and other studies attempting to pin down Cleopatra's ethnicity and skin color. What is motivating all of this? Comparing Cleopatra to the other Egyptians within Handel's opera—who are universally marked as "deceitful" barbarians—we can understand how she remains marked ethnically and socially despite the opera's portrayal of her within the gendered framework of ancient Roman mythology.

Assignment

Have students read from the libretto, the specific scenes related to Cleopatra's character:

- Act I: sc. 5, sc. 7
- Act II: **sc. 1–3, sc. 7–8**
- Act III: **sc. 2–3**, sc. 6, sc. 9

Note: the scenes in boldface would be most important for beginning or intermediate students; if only one group of scenes can be studied, prioritize the famous Act II, sc. 1–3. Instructors can use the scenes in boldface to introduce students to the following conventional scene types in baroque opera—Act II, sc. 1–3: recitativo accompagnato, sinfonia, da capo aria (and its manipulation); Act II, sc. 7–8: sleep scene, pastoral scene; Act III, sc. 2–3: lament.

For discussion in class, ask students to identify examples of "exotic" or gendered representation, and to find ways that the music might (or might not) enhance those portrayals.

Class Activity

Distribute a handout with passages from ancient texts representing Cleopatra. Some good choices to include are excerpts from: Plutarch, "Antony," *Parallel Lives*, Bk. 9, Ch. XXV–XVII, XXIX, XXXVII, LXXI, LXXXVI.[9]

- Either in groups or in a "think-pair-share" exercise, have students identify places where remnants of the ancient representations reappear in the libretto of Handel's opera. (To save time, each group can work on one or two separate text excerpts.)
  - Which characteristics in the ancient text tend to discredit Cleopatra, mark her as a threat, or represent gendered stereotypes?
  - How do ancient politics continue to influence Handel's eighteenth-century opera?
- Watch at least one or two opera videos of Act II, sc. 2.
  - How do the productions differ?
  - Are there aspects of the representation that are surprising?
  - How do the productions portray Cleopatra with respect to the European or "Egyptian" traditions?
- Compare the modern productions to early modern European art; are there parallels, or differences? Some good examples include:
  - ancient coins portraying Cleopatra as Isis;
  - Cleopatra as Venus Genetrix or Venus Anadyomene, as in: Pietro da Cortona, *Caesar giving Cleopatra the throne of Egypt* (c. 1637);
  - Cleopatra as Luxuria, as in: Jacob Jordaens, *Banquet of Cleopatra* (1653)

> **Analysis: Musical Forms, Musical Rhetoric**
>
> This final step can take place in class (if there is time) or can be assigned as an at-home analysis for discussion at the start of the following class period. Beginning students will need some preparation in class ahead of time to be able to recognize the musical features on their own.
>
> - Study the musical forms used in one or more of the assigned scenes.
> - Discuss the roles of sight and sound in the text and music. To what extent is Julius Caesar influenced by Cleopatra's physical appearance versus the sound of her voice?
> - In Act II, sc. 2, how do the disruptions of the audience's expectations signify Cleopatra's difference?
>
> **Analysis: Race and Representation**
>
> As an optional final step, the class could consider how Cleopatra is represented in other media formats today; students could do some additional searching using social media, blog posts, or other popular media to locate representative examples for sharing with the class.
> - Discussion Questions, or Writing Prompts:
>   - How have we racialized Cleopatra in the modern world?
>   - What are the ramifications for opera or other dramatic performances (casting, staging, sets, costuming, gestures, makeup)?
>   - What rhetorical language is being used to discuss Cleopatra in modern media?

Through analytical questions and exercises, students will learn about the textual and visual representation of an ancient figure, tracing similar tropes and narratives from the ancient world through the early modern (and modern) eras, while confronting why and how our discourse about Cleopatra, her "race," and her skin color have become contested issues. Since these questions engage textual and musical analysis, this case study also highlights the continuing importance of traditional musicological skills in the service of new methodologies. Although Cleopatra is not racially marked in Handel's opera, she is marked by gendered and ethnic stereotypes; because our modern world has created racialized discourse around Cleopatra and her representation, Handel's opera becomes an entry point into these discussions. Once students have gained the skills to recognize the early modern representations of "otherness," they will be prepared to analyze the more racially marked depictions in other baroque music dramas, such as Jean-Philippe Rameau's *Les indes galantes* (1735). (See Chapter 3, Case Study 6.)

Case Study 5: Scott Joplin's *Treemonisha* (1911)—African-American Concerns in the "Progressive Era"

Operas by Black composers are noticeably absent in music history survey textbooks; this is a problem resulting from historical and modern bias. Since African Americans, historically, have had smaller professional networks and fewer opportunities for financial or other material support enabling their large-scale works to be performed, their compositions faced a higher barrier to inclusion in the performance canon. Since academic music history was founded originally on European centric repertories, later expanding to include the most widely performed works in European and American performance halls, a significant origin myth/shadow history has developed around Blackness and opera. As a result, students who are interested in African-American music and in opera or musical theater tend to gravitate immediately toward George Gershwin's (1898–1937) *Porgy and Bess* (1935) due to the composer's depiction of Black culture and use of African-American folk genres. This is a grave indicator of how little exposure the average music student has had to Black opera before arriving at college—or even graduate school. The remedy for this is to de-center Gershwin and to re-center Black opera in the classroom. (See Box 2.4.)

In order to fully appreciate Joplin's *Treemonisha*, your students will need a thorough introduction to the development of African-American folk musics and narrative genres, such as the ring shout, the cakewalk, the blues, ragtime, and jazz. Once students are familiar with these idioms, they can begin to recognize how Joplin wove these characteristics into his opera to depict the conflicts between traditional and modern aspects of Black life in America at the turn of the twentieth century.

Repertory

The following set pieces from *Treemonisha*, with related musical examples and reading excerpts, can serve as a focal point for group or individual analysis exercises, completed either in class or as an assignment:

- Act I, no. 4, "We're Goin' Round"

    Traditional Genre: Ring Play or Ring Shout
    Compare: "Blow Gabriel" (several online performances by the McIntosh County Shouters are available)
    Related Reading: Govenar (p. 5), and Vallée (p. 442)

- Act II, no. 11, "Superstition"

Traditional Genre: Blues; Field Hollers, Moans
Compare: Lizzie Miles, "Shootin' Star Blues" (1928)
Related Reading: Vallée (pp. 271–72), Sears (p. 106)

- Act III, no. 21, "Treemonisha's Return"

  Traditional Genre: Field Hollers, Work Songs
  Compare: "Rosie" and "Levee Camp Holler" (recorded by Alan Lomax at Parchman Farm, Mississippi State Penitentiary, 1947–1948)
  Related Readings: Sears (p. 6), Vallée (p. 286)

Reading and Listening Assignment

Students read Ann Sears, "Political Currents and Black Culture in Scott Joplin's *Treemonisha*" and listen to each of the numbers listed above as preparation for the in-class discussion (additional excerpts discussed in Sears could be added for more advanced courses). Sears' discussion of *Treemonisha*'s performance history tells us a lot about the place of Joplin and other Black composers in early twentieth-century music. Have students think about the process of getting an opera performed. what are the challenges?

Class Activity

Step 1: Before class, create handouts with the libretto, score, and reading excerpts for each of the examples listed above, creating three packets—one for each group (make duplicates). At the beginning of class, have students listen (briefly) to each of the assigned *Treemonisha* excerpts followed by its paired musical comparison(s). Students should take notes on the musical style, form, and characteristics of each example while listening; after each paired comparison, have students call out their ideas (briefly) and list them on the board, for later reference. Listening intently together, first, will help students understand the textual and musical components (and how they link to the narrative) before they are influenced by the visual aspects of the staged production and its creative interpretation.

Step 2: In pairs or small groups, students focus on one example packet; their instructions are to elaborate on the initial musical ideas generated by the class, comparing their own analyses to the related reading on the handout packet they received for their specific example. At the conclusion of the group work, each group shares their outcomes in a mini-presentation for the whole class.

> Step 3: After each group shares their ideas, play the corresponding scene from the video production by Houston Grand Opera; have students comment on aspects of the interpretation. This chapter discusses some alternative ways to structure this material either in class, or as an at-home analytical paper.

When using class time for a workshop activity, I give students a target amount of time to spend on each step (5–10 minutes each). I also emphasize that they do not need to have found every possible response; if they have one, two, or three ideas, that will be sufficient. It is fine to move on to the next step even if the group has not "finished" the current step. Moving forward helps students understand where their strengths are, and which skills they may need to focus on improving, while not getting "stuck" or frustrated.

Giving students the freedom to explore ideas without the pressure of having a "perfect" answer can also lead to more vibrant and varied discussions when reconvening with the full group. Questions, peer learning, and collaborative teaching are more likely to arise when we do not all have the same answers, and when we are free to admit that we were not sure about our process or results. During the exercise, I spend time with each group, ensuring that everyone understands the instructions, answering any questions that arise, and working together with them. I complete one step with each group, moving to a new group when it is time to shift focus to the next step in the exercise.

Hybrid In-Class/At-Home Structure

To save class time, the instructor may wish to begin the exercise in class by only completing the first listening exercise together, using just one musical example, and having students do some follow-up reading and a brief analysis paper (c. 500 words) for homework. In this scenario, the instructor might give students a choice of which of the additional examples to focus on for homework, assign specific examples (to ensure even distribution among the class), or have everyone work on the same example. There are many possibilities here, and instructors should feel free to mix things up, to choose the structure that works best for their students or preferred teaching methods, or to fit the amount of time they have available.

In this hybrid in-class/at-home assignment structure, the analysis paper completed at home might serve as a "ticket to enter" class the following instruction day. In this case, each student would bring a printed version of their analysis paper to share with another student at the beginning of class, to trade feedback and ideas. Then each pair would share the main topics they discussed with the full class (total: 15–20 minutes).

The "ticket to enter" strategy maintains accountability and ensures students are ready for active discussion when they arrive to the classroom. At the end of the class period, instructors can collect the printed assignment for a low-stakes grade such as attendance or participation credits (if these are included in your course grading). Using such activities for participation credit is a good way to ensure that students who do not always feel comfortable speaking up in front of the whole class still have a mechanism to demonstrate their knowledge of the material and to influence the overall discussion through their pairs or small groups. It can be useful if students who volunteer to share group ideas in discussion are required to cite the ideas shared by their groupmates. If instructors do not wish to grade these short analysis and discussion assignments, they are still useful to collect and read to get a sense of how individual students are progressing with the material. Then, if the instructor notices any similarities in challenges faced by students, these can be addressed in future class days as a "just-in-time" teaching strategy.

Steppingstones for Research

If the course requires a research project or creative capstone, these in-class activities can be used to teach and frame the relevant research and writing skills. For example, once students have been asked to complete an analysis and discussion assignment on Joplin's *Treemonisha*, they can then locate bibliography materials to contextualize their analysis with scholarship and historical narratives. Often, students start their research project by reading the bibliography and taking notes, but then are stumped with the analysis, or with creating an original hypothesis. Encouraging students to analyze first helps them to create more original projects; as a result, they will begin learning how to create a dialogue with previous scholarship in their writing, instead of stitching together a series of quotations from their sources. (Starting with the analysis can also deter plagiarism, especially in the age of ChatGPT.) After they have completed these steps, they will be ready to realize a similar comparative analysis on a topic of their own choosing, that would form the first stages of their research project (or creative capstone) as a partial rough draft. In this way, students are modeling skills that will directly impact their final learning outcomes. It is a good idea, throughout the semester, to show students how the skills they are developing in class will support other aspects of their education, their creativity, and their independent projects.

A Postscript on George Gershwin

I want to be clear that I do not discourage students from studying Gershwin, even if they want to write a research paper on *Porgy and Bess* in the context of an African-American music class. Some may be surprised by this.

Identity in Historical Narratives 33

However, I *do* require students to engage with the primary sources surrounding Gershwin's folk opera, to interpret them using the tenets of critical race theory (for graduate students), and to understand how the characters map onto (or at least engage with) stereotypical portrayals of Blackness as part of their project. In this way, students learn how origin myths and shadow histories operate together through music performance, pedagogy, and historiography.

Similarly, if instructors want to teach Gershwin, I recommend that they do so from the perspective of origin myths and shadow histories. Start with the shadow history; reveal the full number of African-American operas that were composed prior to Gershwin (and beyond), and discuss the challenges faced by the composers as evidenced in the publication record: scores, performance histories, reviews, recordings, and scholarly research. (See Box 2.4.) Only discuss Gershwin after completing an in-depth study of Joplin's *Treemonisha*. Students should only engage with *Porgy and Bess* after gaining a thorough understanding of Black folk music and African-American compositional achievements in opera and musical theater prior to Gershwin. Then, study *Porgy and Bess* using the "Origin Myths and Shadow Histories" framework. Since this work is now so popular, students should realize that African-American critics were not supportive of Gershwin initially; their critiques were formed due to the dynamics of cultural appropriation and lack of recognition given to existing Black composers—who had already combined African-American folk musics with classical forms (as influenced by Joplin and the Harlem Renaissance).

Box 2.4: Lecture Idea, Research Project—African-American Singers and Composers of Opera

There is a long history of African-American opera singers and composers. Too often, we are conditioned to believe that the "first [fill in the blank]" is also the "only." To rectify this misperception, I encourage instructors to construct a unit or module (using the layered pathway approach; see Chapter 1) that precedes Scott Joplin's *Treemonisha*; begin with a comprehensive overview of African-American singers and composers of opera and musical theater. Since *Treemonisha* occurs relatively early in this history, the unit could be organized from Sissieretta Jones (1868–1933) to George Shirley (b. 1934), highlighting composers such as Harry Lawrence Freeman (1869–1945), Shirley Graham DuBois (1896–1977), and William Grant Still.

Expand this idea for an opera literature survey course. Assign roles and operas performed by African-American singers, via historical images, recordings, or videos (i.e., expanding inclusivity to supporting instructional materials). As an additional creative capstone to the unit, create roundtables organized around central composers or works; each roundtable group assigns one reading to the class in advance. Each student in the group gives a presentation on a short topic, focused on one methodology (biography, musical analysis, cultural themes, dramatic representation of characters and identities, origin myths, etc.). The resulting group presentation thus elucidates shadow histories. After each five-to-ten-minute focused presentation, the class would have five minutes to respond and ask follow-up questions.

Classroom Activity: George Gershwin and His Singers

If you are interested in teaching *Porgy and Bess* due to its modern-day popularity, it is important to also discuss the work's problems from the perspective of racial and cultural representation. Students need to be guided regarding the issues inherent in having cultural stories told by people who are not members of that culture. Have students read primary sources (reviews, interviews) surrounding the premiere of the work, and critique these for stereotypes, bias, and patronizing language. For example, an article by the composer in the *New York Times* (October 30, 1935) displays several concerning stereotypes revealing how he viewed his singers and their culture, for example that "We were able to find these people because what we wanted from them lies in their race" and that "Negroes, as a race,...express themselves not only by the spoken word but quite naturally by song and dance." Some students will not observe these as stereotypes but as "compliments." It is important, therefore, to guide students to critiquing each individual part of the sentence (for example, "as a race" or "quite naturally") for generalizations, and for fallacies in logic. What if the term "Negroes" were substituted for another identity group? How ludicrous would it suddenly be if the sentence were about "women"? Or "men"? Have students identify why that would feel uncomfortable.

The following discussion could emphasize how all forms of art are culturally learned and studied, thus requiring talent, technique, practice, and hard work. Why do we never assume that Western music "comes naturally" to performers of Johann Sebastian Bach and Ludwig van Beethoven, for example? Another important aspect of Black culture that can be read through Gershwin's comments about his singers (in other sources) is how he had to instruct them to learn the dialect that supposedly represented "their culture." What does this mean about "authenticity" of representation within *Porgy and Bess*? Why do we assume that there is only "one way" or "one dialect" or "one accent" that applies to all Black Americans? How should we perform this work today? How do we handle language and diction?

Analyze gestures in staged performances. How much autonomy do African-American singers have in portraying these characters, and how related are they to minstrelsy stereotypes that were prevalent in Gershwin's time? Some questions will be more relevant to advanced students of singing or opera, but all of them can lead to greater understanding of historical racial and cultural origin myths, how they are embedded in cultural products, and how we engage with them today.

With these challenging conversations, instructors will need to be prepared for students who have been so acculturated to stereotypical or demeaning portrayals of African Americans that they will not see the problems indicated here. For this reason, I have a blanket policy in my classes that disagreements are not ever to be made in statements, but in questions. This allows learning to occur while protecting respectful dialogue. Be aware not to make African-American students "stand in" as representatives of Black culture or explain what racism looks and feels like. As an instructor, if you are not prepared to understand these issues from the perspectives outlined here—and to respond firmly but comfortably to students who ask uncomfortable questions—then do not do this classroom activity, and I also respectfully urge you not to assign Gershwin's *Porgy and Bess*.

Notes

1 Since this is the term most frequently used to describe the traditional "canon" taught in music history classrooms in the U.S., Europe, and elsewhere, I am using it in this book; however, I recognize the inadequacy of this term, as my goal is to push beyond and redefine how this subject is taught. I note that "Western" is problematic, since it emphasizes a colonial viewpoint, mostly to distinguish certain repertories originating in Europe and its North American colonies, and those taught under the rubric of "musicology" versus "ethnomusicology." "Art" is problematic, since it implies that other forms of music are not "artistic," or "cultivated," or of high socio-economic value. Despite the problematic aspects of this term, there is no consensus on a replacement within academic circles. Thus, I encourage instructors to have discussions with their students surrounding this and similar terms, such as "classical music," or "concert music" and to always re-define terminology based on specific musical historical circumstances. The frameworks advanced in this book can be used to uncover inequities and promote musical inclusiveness when applied to any musics under discussion.
2 Edward W. Said, *Beginnings: Intention and Method* (New York: Columbia University Press, 1985).
3 For more detail on my definitions of origin myths and shadow histories, see Smith, "EDITORIAL."
4 Kyle Adams, "What Did Danger Mouse Do? The Grey Album and Musical Composition in Configurable Culture," *Music Theory Spectrum* 37, no. 1 (2015): 7–24.
5 Fabrice Fitch, *Renaissance Polyphony*, 1., Cambridge Introductions to Music (New York: Cambridge University Press, 2020).
6 Jesse Rodin, "'When in Rome......': What Josquin Learned in the Sistine Chapel," *Journal of the American Musicological Society* 61, no. 2 (August 1, 2008): 307–72, https://doi.org/10.1525/jams.2008.61.2.307.
7 See Ralph P. Locke, *Music and the Exotic from the Renaissance to Mozart* (New York; Cambridge: Cambridge University Press, 2015) for some of the challenges with defining "exoticism" in this repertory.

36 *Identity in Historical Narratives*

8 Daniel Hershenzon, *The Captive Sea: Slavery, Communication, and Commerce in Early Modern Spain and the Mediterranean* (Philadelphia: University of Pennsylvania Press, 2018), https://doi.org/10.9783/9780812295368.
9 Plutarch, *Plutarch's Lives: With an English Translation by Bernadotte Perrin, in Eleven Volumes*, trans. Bernadotte Perrin, vol. IX, The Loeb Classical Library 101 (London: William Heinemann, 1920).

Annotated Bibliography

Origin Myths and Shadow Histories

Hershenzon, Daniel. *The Captive Sea: Slavery, Communication, and Commerce in Early Modern Spain and the Mediterranean.* Philadelphia: University of Pennsylvania Press, 2018. https://doi.org/10.9783/9780812295368.

I recommend the "Introduction" (pp. 1–16) for instructors wishing to contextualize the role of captivity, conversion, forced labor, imprisonment, and ransom in the early modern Mediterranean world; this book is also helpful for understanding the economic, political, religious, and social interconnectivity between Christians, Jews, and Muslims during this period. It is important to note that this book is not about race; in fact, the Mediterranean slave practices removed certain distinctions between race and class that would have operated in captives' lives prior to their captivity; one European captive described being marched to the slave market as becoming a "new black [person]" (p. 22). This statement also indicates that the "status" of a person who has been devalued is equated with being Black. Although there are some brief comparisons to the Atlantic slave trade (which was distinctly racialized), it is important to be aware that this is not the main subject of this book. Therefore, instructors wishing to understand race, slavery, and the Atlantic slave world should seek out other sources. It would not be a good idea to allow comparisons between these distinctly different systems to enter classroom discussion, since these also resulted in different social and economic outcomes within the modern world.

Said, Edward W. *Beginnings: Intention and Method.* New York: Columbia University Press, 1985.

Although postcolonial theory can often be dense and challenging to read (especially for undergraduates), Said is quite accessible. I recommend this book for instructors who want to begin thinking differently about how we construct histories; instructors may wish to assign a chapter or two to advanced undergraduate or graduate students.

Sensitive and Harmful Language

These three thoughtful articles could be assigned to advanced undergraduate and graduate students as a follow-up to your course policies about language usage:

Price, Sean. "Straight Talk about the N-Word." *Learning for Justice*, no. 40 (2011). https://www.learningforjustice.org/magazine/fall-2011/straight-talk-about-the-nword.
Southgate, Martha. "Teaching the History of Racist Language." *Grécourt Gate: News and Events for the Smith College Community*, March 17, 2021. https://www.smith.edu/news/2021-saq-sp-prof-elizabeth-stordeur-pryor-n-word.

"We Have Waited Long Enough: Black Students' Response to CCSRE Faculty Directors." *The Stanford Daily*, May 31, 2020. https://stanforddaily.com/2020/05/31/we-have-waited-long-enough-black-students-response-to-ccsre-faculty-directors/#disqus_thread.

Motets and Mashups

Adams, Kyle. "What Did Danger Mouse Do? The *Grey Album* and Musical Composition in Configurable Culture." *Music Theory Spectrum* 37, no. 1 (2015): 7–24.

Reviews various mashup structures, comparing them to earlier compositional approaches such as organum, musical borrowing, jazz "cutting contests," collage, and *musique concrète* (pp. 7–12). The middle section of the article provides detailed analysis of three mashups by Danger Mouse from *The Grey Album*: "99 Problems," "What More Can I Say," and "Change Clothes;" this section could be assigned to advanced undergraduates (pp. 13–19), or instructors could use one or more of the musical examples to build a lecture. The final section questions the definitions of material, tools, interpretation, performance, and composition (pp. 19–23); instructors could use these as discussion questions in class, after studying various works that re-use musical materials from differing styles and historical periods.

Briscoe, James R., ed. *New Historical Anthology of Music by Women*. Bloomington: Indiana University Press, 2004.

A good resource for finding scores by women composers; useful as a textbook for classes with significant emphasis on women composers in different eras. Contains motets and madrigals for study materials or analysis assignments. Since it can sometimes be challenging to find both a score and a good recording for the same work, instructors might pair two different pieces by the same composer. For example, the *Anthology* includes Maddalena Casulana's "Morte, che voi," which is good for score study and analysis, and can be paired with Casulana's "Morir non può il mio core," which has been recorded by the Hilliard Ensemble. (See Box 2.2, 2.3, Figure 2.1.)

Elders, Willem. *Josquin Des Prez and His Musical Legacy: An Introductory Guide*. Revised and Translated edition. Leuven: Leuven University Press, 2013.

A reference source for lecture preparation on Josquin biography, authorship issues, compositional style, and analysis. Some sections could be suitable for reading assignments.

Fitch, Fabrice. *Renaissance Polyphony*. 1. Cambridge Introductions to Music. New York: Cambridge University Press, 2020.

Provides a thorough background on all aspects of Renaissance polyphony, from theoretical concepts to the historical contexts of musical creators, and how the music functions in sacred and secular spaces, as well as analysis of specific works. (See Box 2.1, 2.2, Figure 2.1.)

Parsons, Laurel, and Brenda Ravenscroft, eds. *Analytical Essays on Music by Women Composers: Secular & Sacred Music to 1900*. Vol. 1. Oxford University Press, 2018. https://doi.org/10.1093/oso/9780190237028.001.0001.

38 Identity in Historical Narratives

This book is a great resource for exploring the theoretical complexity and rhetorical meaning of music by women—which counterbalances the traditional focus on women's lives and biographical writing in music history. The first three chapters (beyond the Introduction) discuss Hildegard of Bingen, Maddalena Casulana, and Barbara Strozzi; instructors can use these to develop theoretical concepts from the medieval through baroque eras. These are especially useful when instructors introduce a musical concept and ask students to use that concept in their own analysis as a group exercise in class or as a take-home assignment; then, they are more prepared to be able to read one of the analytical chapters on the same or similar topics. (See Box 2.1, 2.2, 2.3, Figure 2.1.)

Rodin, Jesse. "'When in Rome......': What Josquin Learned in the Sistine Chapel." *Journal of the American Musicological Society* 61, no. 2 (August 1, 2008): 307–72. https://doi.org/10.1525/jams.2008.61.2.307.

Contains many interesting examples that instructors can draw upon to illustrate the importance of place, biography, and musical influence—and, how these factors can shape our understanding of a composer's style, ultimately altering historiography.

George Frideric Handel's Giulio Cesare (1724)

Locke, Ralph P. *Music and the Exotic from the Renaissance to Mozart*. New York; Cambridge: Cambridge University Press, 2015.

The first two chapters ("Introduction" and "Exotic in Style?") explain the terminology, methods, and principles of the book. I recommend assigning some excerpts of these to students, in combination with some short analytical exercises to help them evaluate their own recognition of various types of identity representation in operatic scenes, whether in the primary textual and musical sources or in modern performance videos. Locke does upend our typical notions of the meaning of the word "exoticism" (see esp. pp. 3–9); he considers modern performance issues on pp. 11–16. The second chapter goes deeper into Locke's methods for determining the presence of exoticism (see esp. pp. 17–26 and 28–40).

Scott Joplin's Treemonisha (1911)

Govenar, Alan B. *Texas Blues: The Rise of a Contemporary Sound*. College Station: Texas A & M University Press, 2008. http://site.ebrary.com/id/10447178.

The section on slave narratives about music in Texas offers first-hand descriptions of music-making related to the ring shout (pp. 3–6). This section also has background on West African musical instruments similar to the banjo, which contributed to early African-American blues traditions. This material can be used in comparison with *Treemonisha* Act I, sc. 4. (see Case Study 5.) The cited primary narratives and the images of Black musicians from the past and the present can generate additional discussion. Students should be encouraged to consider the fallacies—and implicit bias—underlying comparisons of ancient cultures to modern day folk cultures.

Maultsby, Portia K., and Mellonee V. Burnim. *Issues in African American Music: Power, Gender, Race, Representation*. Abingdon, Oxfordshire: Routledge, 2017. https://doi.org/10.4324/9781315472096.

Excellent critical essays covering the major genres of African-American music and related critical methodologies. Readings will be useful for both instructors and students. For familiarizing students with the background materials on early African-American music, I especially recommend the following chapters: Chapter 19: "The Antebellum Period: Communal Coherence and Individual Expression," (pp. 331–42, by Lawrence W. Levine); Chapter 14: "Women in Blues: Transgressing Boundaries" (pp. 237–55, by Daphne Duval Harrison); Chapter 1: "Performing Blues and Navigating Race in Transcultural Contexts" (pp. 3–29); and Chapter 2: "New Bottle, Old Wine: Whither Jazz Studies?" (pp. 30–46, by Travis A. Jackson).

Rosenbaum, Art, Margo Newmark Rosenbaum, and Johann S. Buis. *Shout Because You're Free: The African American Ring Shout Tradition in Coastal Georgia*; [Twenty-Five Shout Songs as Sung by the McIntosh County Shouters]. Paperback ed. Athens; London: University of Georgia Press, 2013. Includes "Blow Gabriel" (see Case Study 5).

Sears, Ann. "Political Currents and Black Culture in Scott Joplin's Treemonisha." In *Blackness in Opera*, edited by Naomi André, Karen M. Bryan, and Eric Saylor. Urbana: University of Illinois Press, 2017. https://doi.org/10.5406/illinois/9780252036781.003.0006.

This chapter reviews Joplin's biography and the performance history of *Treemonisha*, including the composer's difficulties with receiving support for the work. Sears also includes an overview of the plot and musical styles, with close analysis of how *Treemonisha* represents Black identity in the early twentieth-century U.S., and how it responds to the educational philosophies of Booker T. Washington (1865–1915) and W.E.B. DuBois (1868–1963). This chapter is a good assignment for introducing students to the opera before beginning the analytical exercises described in Case Study 5.

Vallée, Elisabet Omarene de. "Building Blocks of a National Style: An Examination of Topics and Gestures in Nineteenth-Century American Music as Exemplified in Scott Joplin's Treemonisha." PhD diss., University of Northern Colorado, 2017. https://www.proquest.com/pagepdf/1970167700?accountid=10226.

This dissertation contains many musical comparisons between Joplin's opera and traditional African-American music; although some of these comparisons can be critiqued, students can learn how to use critique in research writing by creating their own analyses (as described in Case Study 5) and comparing them to Vallée's work.

3 Representational Tropes in Text, Image, and Music

The "Mimesis to Mockery" framework introduced in this chapter instructs readers to recognize various rhetorical strategies of representation, ranging from the seemingly harmless to the obviously caricaturized. Using a scale from invisibility to hypervisibility (drawing from critical race theory), this framework demonstrates how mimesis, mockery, and everything in-between overlap with exoticism—while also showing how exoticism is an inadequate tool for understanding the complex representation of identity in Western art music.[1] (See Figure 3.1.)

Although I am drawing from some basic tenets of critical race theory here,[2] I want to emphasize that it is not necessary to have expertise in this specialized field to use the "Mimesis to Mockery" framework as an analytical methodology, as it stands on its own. The "Mimesis to Mockery" framework has the additional advantage of being applicable to any representational, hierarchical power dynamic regardless of the specific identities involved. Because critical race theory was developed specifically to highlight the historical and legal dimensions of how African-American identity functions in the U.S., its principles do not necessarily transfer to other situations without significant adjustments; therefore, it is not always helpful for discussing art music created in Europe that portrays other marginalized identities. The "Mimesis to Mockery" framework offers greater flexibility, allowing representational nuances regarding a multitude of identities (disability, ethnicity, gender, nationality, etc.) to become legible in a variety of genres.

The framework begins with the overarching concept that representation can either make an identity appear invisible, or hypervisible. While these terms are used in critical race theory, they also existed prior to and outside of it. Outside of critical race theory, hypervisibility has been used as an analytical concept in art and literature since the 1980s. Prior to critical race theory, invisibility has been used as an analytical concept in ethnographic/folklore studies, philosophy, psychology, and religious studies since the early twentieth century. In literature, Ralph Ellison famously uses invisibility as a metaphor for race relations in the U.S. in his 1952 novel, *Invisible Man*. Because critical race theory levies these analytical terms toward law and society, with implications for education and culture at large, I acknowledge the field's influence on

DOI: 10.4324/9781003219385-3

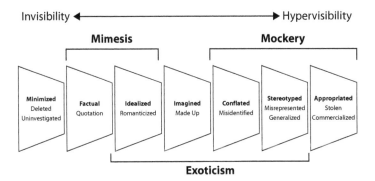

Figure 3.1 **From Mimesis to Mockery.** On a spectrum from invisibility to hypervisibility, representational types or categories can be mimetic or mocking of identity and culture, overlapping in some ways, but not fully, with conventional definitions of exoticism.

my framework here. However, for those who do not have enough background in critical race theory to feel comfortable using it, be assured that you do not need any additional materials beyond what I include in this chapter to benefit from the "Mimesis to Mockery" framework in scholarship and teaching. (For using critical race theory in an instructional context, see Box 3.1.)

Box 3.1: Lecture, Discussion, and Analysis—Critical Race Theory

For those interested in exploring critical race theory in the classroom, I recommend assigning the Ladson-Billings and Tate article (Ladson-Billings and Tate 1995). I ask students to identify 3–5 concepts or historical scenarios that were new to them, identify their meaning, and write a paragraph about their significance historically, in the present, and in music studies. After discussing their responses in class, students then use their chosen terms to analyze their next reading and repertory assignment.

In my graduate level African-American music class, this worked well for analyzing the racial dynamics surrounding the birth of the concert spiritual through the Fisk Jubilee Singers. Students read Chapter 2 (pp. 26–49) and Chapter 3 from Graham (2018).

In Figure 3.1, the spectrum from invisibility (being minimized, ignored, deleted, unacknowledged, or left out) to hypervisibility (being overly "policed," aggressed, stereotyped, or culturally appropriated) encompasses many underlying and interlocking mechanisms of representation that are common in both historical and contemporary cultural products. The "Mimesis to Mockery" framework is most easily applied to forms of music drama, since they combine image, text, and music, as shown in Case Study 6, with imagination and creativity. This framework also suits instrumental music analysis, as demonstrated in Case Study 7.

Mimesis (representation or imitation) is the primary mechanism through which art, literature, music, and theater provide meaning to an audience. As the subject of much philosophical debate regarding "truth" or "verisimilitude" in representation from Plato to the present, mimesis is the foundation of each era's aesthetic tastes and stylistic development in musical language and related arts. Whereas ancient Greeks believed that different musical modes could represent character or ethnicity (and could thus impact the actions and behaviors of the listener), the Romantics believed that music could outwardly imitate an internal, self-reflexive, emotional life.

Theories of mimesis are foundational to the historical development of opera from Claudio Monteverdi to Christoph Willibald Gluck, Richard Wagner, and beyond. Because of its prevalence in scholarship on art history, literature, music, and philosophy, mimesis is argued about in idealized, positive terms. Musicologists tend to think of mimesis as a sonic attempt to represent experiences that approximate the real world presented through fictionalized layers. In other words, the scholarly trajectory about mimesis traces composers' different methods for trying to get closer to the truth. But mimesis can also incorporate untruthful, damaging, or offensive forms of imitation. As Figure 3.1 shows, idealized or romanticized imitations of other cultures can verge on exoticism, and when exoticism moves through the spectrum toward hypervisibility, it becomes more negatively charged. It is from this vantage point that I developed the "Mimesis to Mockery" framework.

When authors or artists conflate, misidentify, misrepresent, or stereotype others for the purposes of commercial entertainment, they offer audiences "pleasure" and "instruction/enlightenment;" these are the commonly accepted goals for mimetic performance, going back to Horace's well-known mandate, *placere et docere* (to please and instruct), from the *Ars poetica (Art of poetry)*. When pleasure, instruction, or enlightenment happen through demeaning gestures, there are significant ramifications for identity and society. In Figure 3.1, I use the term "mockery" to distinguish explicitly harmful types of representation from the more seemingly harmless forms of mimesis. Please note, however, that the absence of representation—the strongest form of invisibility—is also a harmful area, despite being on the opposite end of the spectrum from hypervisibility. By placing mimesis and mockery inside the broader spectrum of invisibility and hypervisibility, I argue that we do not have to accept all forms of representation or imitation just because there is a long-held, respectable, and philosophically oriented set of academic disciplines that engage with theorizing of mimesis. We should clearly demarcate forms of mimesis that uplift, from those that degrade.

Figure 3.1 also demonstrates how exoticism sits uncomfortably between mimesis and mockery; however, exoticism alone does not define the full range of representational paradigms, tropes, or stereotypes that can be present on the scale from invisibility to hypervisibility with respect to "othered" representations. Exoticism always involves cultural distance and foreignness, encompassing a range from idealization, romanticization, and imagination, to conflation and stereotypical misrepresentation. Although these levels may not be intrinsically negative or harmful, when representations that idealize, romanticize, and invent identity characteristics, are simultaneously imbued with exoticism, they can double the potential for implicit bias or for cultural misrepresentation to emerge. Thus, the overlapping areas between exoticism and mimesis—or between exoticism and otherwise neutrally positioned "imagined" fictions—can become fraught and should be studied more closely. These areas may not be as overt in their distortion as the more strongly mocking representations, but they can still be problematic.

For these reasons, approaches within musicology that treat cultural difference in representational forms as "exoticism" (and its corollaries in postcolonial scholarship) are not sufficient to undo origin myths. Essentially, these forms of scholarship continue to point at origin myths, possibly calling them out and making them visible, but do not undo their power or their hold over us; only uncovering shadow histories can do that. This chapter, and the remaining chapters in this book, each provide frameworks to deconstruct, uncover, and disempower origin myths so that we can make more visible the shadow histories that they obscure. Making the shadows more visible prevents hypervisibility (which develops from lack of knowledge). Removing power from hypervisibility prevents stereotypes from taking root and gaining control in our cultural consciousness and cultural discourses.

What about "parody" and "satire"? This is a question I have received in response to my "Mimesis to Mockery" framework. Parody and satire always encompass some grain of truth at their core, by posing a recognizable scenario, situation, or custom at the center of the fiction, thus enabling the audience to identify with the subject of ridicule. It is precisely this juxtaposition between the true and the outrageously untrue, producing the desired comedic effect, that prevents these genres from holding a position further toward the "factual" end of the mimesis spectrum. Since these genres have the same narrative goal as "idealization," it might be reasonable to place them directly in the middle of the spectrum, right between "idealized" and "imagined" as shown in Figure 3.1. The purpose of these comedic categories of representation is to show what *should* be "ideal," based on portraying what is decidedly—and ridiculously—*not* ideal. Paradoxically, it is also this core of supposedly inherent truthfulness contained in parody and satire that prevents them from eclipsing the boundaries of "imagined," "invented," or "made up"—no matter how outlandish the invented fiction. Thus, we seem to have found a rightful place, one that seems to balance comfortably on the spectrum between mimesis and mockery, and between invisibility and hypervisibility.

So why have I not included parody and satire right in the middle of this spectrum? I have not done so since that would make it seem that a genre closely connected to ridicule is neutral and therefore harmless. These modes can only be neutral when the target of ridicule is directed inwardly within the same culture, organization, or social group as the narrative frame of reference, or when directed outwardly at an identity or group that is equal in status with the narrative frame of reference.

When satire or parody are directed at groups or entities that have less economic, cultural, political, or social status, the representation becomes hypervisible—similar in scale to conflations or stereotypes. Therefore, parody and satire themselves can be multi-layered; within the same work, one group can be targeted as neutral while another group can be targeted as negative. Precisely because these genres work in this way, they are frequently used as "excuses" or "apologies" for sexist, racist, or otherwise demeaning portrayals. If you doubt this analysis, just think about blackface minstrelsy compared to other comedic vaudeville productions. Making fun of cowboys is not the same thing as making "fun" of Indigenous peoples—or of African-American "Mammys" and "Zip Coons." The recognizable "truth" in these parodies is only perceptible to the dominant group that created it, because it represents the so-called "truth" of racism. For the people being "parodied," there is no truth at all, and the representation is harmful.

Although these more negative portrayals are fictional, they are based on common thought patterns that already exist in society; if this were not the case, it would be impossible to identify stereotypes, since every portrayal would be completely unique. Furthermore, as these fictional portrayals gain popular currency, they are repeated continuously, accruing increasing authority. The more these stereotyped representations become cemented in the public's consciousness, the more they are difficult to dislodge. When "othered" groups are repeatedly portrayed in the submissive or negative position—as with certain operatic performances in Western art music—these performances can provide societal acceptance of political actions or social conditions, such as colonialism or discrimination. The very expensive operatic system, historically requiring financial patronage from wealthy donors, lends additional weight to the ways in which those in power can influence the fictional representations enjoyed by the public. This combination can lead to a cycle of dispossession on behalf of the "othered" cultures represented in this genre.

Implications for Research

The framework "Mimesis to Mockery" does not only apply to representations in fictional contexts; it also applies to the ways in which scholarship and historiography study, analyze, represent, and codify musical works into canons and curricula. When we ignore representations of "others" within musical works or musical sources, we create entrenched patterns of historical and scholarly invisibility that endure for generations. The persistence of historians "skipping over" the "uncomfortable bits" of narrative that demonstrate exoticism, mockery, hypervisibility, or racism as thought patterns influencing the worldviews of musicians, theorists, philosophers, performers, etc., while highlighting the parts that scholars deem "more relevant," creates an unbalanced, inaccurate history.

This mechanism is akin to "colorblind racism." By denying the existence of race and racialized discourse (and by extension ethnicity, gender, sexuality, and disability), we sweep it under the rug. The effect, then, creates a shadow history. The remaining perception, as a result, is that these "othered" identity groups did not exist, did not participate, or had no significance. Therefore, the dominant group either wittingly or unwittingly constructs—or is implicitly folded into—the corresponding origin myth. By correlating fictional representations with narrative accounts in primary sources, we can begin to recognize how origin myths developed and how they have been sustained in scholarship, pedagogy, and performance. We also begin to realize that the history of Western music was already a diverse place with many cross-cultural interactions, and that, therefore, people of diverse backgrounds today inherently belong to this long tradition.[3]

In scholarship, the dynamics of invisibility/hypervisibility—either ignoring the representation of race and ethnicity, or focusing on race only within certain contexts (such as exoticism, orientalism, or postcolonial studies)—means that the topic is not "normalized," but becomes the purview of only a selected few. This makes the subject inaccessible to students—and to their instructors seeking solutions to a curriculum that overwhelmingly focuses on the accomplishments of white composers and performers, without addressing the structural barriers that were constructed for those of other backgrounds.

Even using the definition given by Ralph Locke (see Chapters 1 and 2), which significantly expands our understanding of "exoticism," we cannot truly identify how racial and ethnic stereotypes are embedded in cultural practices, since whole swaths of representational categories are not included. Exoticism tends to be linked with gender. Therefore, when we use exoticism as an analytical lens, we are often dissuaded from recognizing how female characters are represented as complying with the norms of the dominant culture to gain acceptance, while male characters are not as frequently presented as objects of desire (an important component of exoticism). Then, we miss the clues to how they are "othered."

Cleopatra in George Frideric Handel's *Giulio Cesare*, who is represented with the symbols of ancient Roman (i.e., "Western") iconography and moral decorum, provides a perfect example of this phenomenon. (See Chapter 2, Case Study 4.) Since Cleopatra is depicted as "normal" according to the values imposed within the opera, she cannot be "exotic." We do not perceive her as ethnically or racially marked in the text, except once we realize that "deception"—a negative trait associated with the other Egyptians in the opera—is the mechanism by which she is able to project and align herself with Roman symbolisms to her own advantage. In other words, without understanding the representational tropes applied throughout the work, we do not realize that the same "barbarous" "treachery" ascribed to all Egyptians is also ascribed to Cleopatra. The origin myth of Cleopatra participating in or belonging to ancient Roman culture is strong. We have been acculturated to that myth through hundreds of years of iconography in art, literature, music, and other media. Without a deep analysis, it is all too easy to dismiss her from a category of being ethnically or racially marked.

Researchers can use the "Mimesis to Mockery" framework to great advantage, while creating new scholarship that makes baroque opera more accessible for pedagogical purposes. One of the disadvantages to postcolonial studies is that instructors generally cannot use the resulting books and articles as classroom material, since they are too complex, too specialized, and require too much background for most undergraduate level reading assignments.

There is no "neutral" representation of minority identities within the structures of early and early modern culture, and these problems continue today through stereotyped media of all sorts. The first steps toward addressing the persistent issues surrounding cultural diversity in our institutions and curricula is recognizing how we ended up where we are today. That process begins with recognizing the tropes and rhetorics involved in the "Mimesis to Mockery" framework, so that we can rectify imbalances and uncover shadow histories. Essentially, representational tropes and stereotypes function as origin myths both in our society, and in our historiography.

Having an objective tool, such as the "Mimesis to Mockery" framework, allows classroom conversations to go beyond the one-dimensional finger-pointing often involved in conversations about race, which center binary thinking such as "this is racist" or "this is not racist," thus leading to further conflict and entrenchment. As soon as one person says "that is so racist" the conversation cannot continue, and those who do not understand or recognize the racial stereotypes—or the historical and present harm those stereotypes have enacted—lose an important learning opportunity. Often, we recognize racisms and other stereotypes by intuition without understanding the why and the how behind those systems. The "Mimesis to Mockery" framework helps instructors and students understand how racism is indeed not a binary system; it is not one thing or another thing but a complex system involving multiple strategies, including patterned and predictable representations of intentionally "othered" identities. Once students can recognize how these systems of representation functioned in the past, they can begin to recognize how those same patterns operate in the present. Researchers can use this framework to expand the analytical options available and gain more creative and diverse results while revealing multi-layered symbolisms within a single work, thereby generating more scholarship that not only advances the field but also informs classroom instruction.

As discussed in Chapter 2, Box 2.5, these conversations must begin with questions—not statements. The case studies here (6 and 7) both juxtapose external stereotypes with internal identity-based experiences as reflected in primary sources by past and present authors. This methodology continues skills practiced in Chapter 2, Case Study 4, on Handel's *Giulio Cesare* ; instructors may wish to employ the "Origin Myths and Shadow Histories" framework associated with Case Study 4 before introducing students to the materials in this chapter.

Case Study 6: Jean-Philippe Rameau, *Nouvelles Suites* (1726–1727), and *Les Indes galantes* (1735)

Jean-Philippe Rameau's mimicry of American Indian dance in his keyboard dance movement "Les Sauvages" from the *Nouvelles Suites* (1726–1727), which he later adapted into a *divertissement* for his opera-ballet *Les Indes galantes* (1735/1736), is one of the most popular French baroque harpsichord pieces in today's performance world.[4] The music is striking and repetitive, making it a crowd pleaser. The narrative behind the work's composition marks a significant historical moment, thus offering great storytelling appeal to audiences. In the classroom, a comparative approach contrasting the harpsichord version with the later orchestrated version that includes vocal strains and dance, seems engaging for teaching history and analysis.

These works raise many problematic challenges, however; if we do not consider the sensitive issues surrounding how Rameau represented Indigenous peoples through gesture, dance, and drama, we might create a painful environment in the classroom. Before we embark on teaching these pieces, we should ask ourselves the following questions: 1) *Should* we be teaching these pieces? 2) If yes, then what are the reasons for doing so? 3) Can we meet the same pedagogical goals using different music? 4) How can we shift our thinking, to redesign how we teach these works? 5) How does this music, and the scholarship on it, convey origin myths? 6) Are there ethical approaches for teaching these works? 7) How do the layers of representation operate on the scale of "mimesis to mockery," in music, performance, and scholarship? 8) If it is important to show a video production of the opéra-ballet, which one is most suitable, and how should the classroom discussion be framed?

Questions 1–3 are perhaps the most important considerations. If the primary reason for teaching these works is to demonstrate the rondeau form in both keyboard and stage dance iterations, there are other pieces that will serve this purpose; in this case, instructors should probably not teach "Les Sauvages." Jean-Baptiste Lully (1632–1687), Antonia Padoani Bembo (1640–1720), Élisabeth Claude Jacquet de la Guerre (1665–1729), and Francois Couperin (1668–1733), all wrote enticing works in rondeau form, whether for harpsichord, voice, or for the dramatic stage. (See Box 3.2, 3.3.) If the primary reason to teach these works is to emphasize Rameau's expanding harpsichord language and technique, or to demonstrate the uniquely French *divertissement*, there are other works by Lully or Rameau that can serve these purposes. (See Box 3.4.)

Box 3.2: Lecture Idea—Élisabeth Claude Jacquet de la Guerre and French Baroque Dance

Teach conventional baroque dance genres through Jacquet de la Guerre's keyboard suites. Several character pieces show her flare for drama and the influence of opera theater on her compositional style. Her piece "La Flamande" or "The Flemish Woman" (*Pièces de clavecin* Bk. 2, "Suite en re mineur," 1707) bears several stylistic features of the *intonazione*, toccata, unmeasured prelude, and allemande (all of which are suitable for the first movement of a keyboard suite), while the halting rhythmic accents might be interpreted as representing the traditional wooden clogs worn in Flanders and the Low Countries.

Encourage students to draw their own analytical conclusions by first teaching them the underlying styles (listed above) through listening examples. Then, have students identify any irregularities in "La Flamande," and draw conclusions about the resulting meaning from the perspective of French court ballet. Watch one or more excerpts of a *divertissement* or *entrée* performed in historical style from a Lully *tragédie en musique* or a Rameau *opéra-ballet*. Depending on the selection chosen, discuss the role of ethnized characters and the use of blackface in seventeenth-century stage drama (See Bloechl 2015, Childs 2017, Ndiaye 2021). Finally, teach students about Jacquet de la Guerre's religious cantatas and her opera *Céphale et Procris* (1694). This class plan teaches students how abstract keyboard music can elicit layers of meaning, how to listen with historical ears, and to appreciate the knowledge that eighteenth-century audiences brought with them to the performance.

> **Box 3.3: Class Activity—Women, Gender, and "Prodigies" in the Eighteenth Century**
>
> In the seventeenth and early eighteenth centuries, the word "prodigy" had a very different meaning; it was not until later (students will recognize the example of Wolfgang Amadeus Mozart) that it was considered important or special to display extraordinary talent at a young age. The celebrity culture of "prodigies" is a relatively modern development. In the early modern era, "prodigy" or "prodigious" were terms applied more to objects and events than to people: comets, falling stars, omens, monsters, etc. We should think carefully, therefore, when women are hailed as "prodigies" in eighteenth-century sources.
>
> In class, have students read brief excerpts from articles or book chapters about eighteenth-century women labeled as "prodigies." Some examples are Laura Bassi (scientist; 1711–1778), Maria Maddalena Morelli (poet, pseud. Corilla Olimpica; 1727–1800), and Raffaella Aleotti (composer and conductor; c. 1570–c. 1646). In small groups, have students identify important or striking aspects of their careers. What factors aided or hindered women's career trajectories? Assign Cyr, Mary. "Elisabeth Jacquet de La Guerre: Myth or Marvel? Seeking the Composer's Individuality." The Musical Times 149, no. 1905 (2008): 79–87. https://doi.org/doi:10.2307/25434573 to prepare this discussion.

It is very important to *not* teach these works if the main reason for doing so is to frame the material as "cross-cultural exchange" or as a "cool" and "surprising" fact that a delegation of American Indian peoples traveled to Paris in the early eighteenth century. If that is the depth of knowledge that we are bringing to the historical context, it is not sufficient for teaching students the role that colonialism, race, ethnicity, politics, and representation played in eighteenth-century music and the development of the Western canon. However, if instructors wish to teach traditional form and analytical skills *and* to teach cultural competency while broadening students' educational experiences, all these goals can be accomplished in an ethical way.

Another reason to teach these works is that students are likely to encounter them in their lifetimes, either as performers or as concertgoers, if they have an interest in early music. They may also encounter written discussions of these pieces that are problematic. We have the opportunity, in the classroom, to use music to teach important critical thinking and analysis skills, to educate students about race and its representation in the world around us, and to push back against harmful representations that students may encounter elsewhere.

To avoid having this class material become the tokenizing "one day that we talk about race" or about Indigenous peoples, I refer instructors to the method described as "layered pathways" in Chapter 1. Preface your discussion with class sessions on colonial music in the Americas, American Indian musical cultures, repertory of the Latin American baroque, early African-American music, and other related topics—such as the differing experiences under French, Spanish, and English colonialism.

Questions 4–6 prompt us to shift our thinking away from the standard narrative about Rameau's "Les Sauvages." Textbooks and other general scholarship on Rameau or baroque music frequently demonstrate the invisibility/hypervisibility levels of engagement outlined in Figure 3.1. Materials that instructors are most likely to use for class preparation or for assigned reading either do not discuss these pieces at all—or do so in ways that are insensitive (at best) to the American Indian cultures that they portray. These books either use terms like "aggressive" to describe the music, conflate or misidentify the delegates who visited Paris, or use apologist arguments to (incorrectly) justify the use of the term "savages" in the titles.

More specialized books and articles on American Indian representation in French baroque opera tend to be less accessible to the classroom, inadvertently and unwittingly contributing to a form of "hypervisibility" in which these works are only discussed from the position of "otherness" in educational contexts. Making these pieces and people "invisible" by not discussing them leads to an origin myth, creating a knowledge vacuum about the role and representation of colonialism and identity in Western art music. Making them "hypervisible" through inaccurate or stereotypical descriptions also contributes to origin myths. This case study gives instructors mechanisms for uncovering shadow histories and opening new layers of interpretation, while making space in the classroom to discuss Indigenous histories through music.

How can we unsettle the one-directional gaze established by Rameau through his musical representations? The only way to do this is to analyze the textual, musical, and imagistic representations, and then to reverse the gaze by identifying and centering Indigenous perspectives as much as possible using available primary sources. While the second step may not be possible within the scope of classroom instruction, it is an approach that researchers can use to enhance existing scholarship.

Lecture Idea

When introducing the *Nouvelles Suites* (1726–27), contextualize the movement "Les Sauvages" by making a list of all the titles and what they represent. (See Figure 3.2.) This could be framed as a class activity, by asking students to listen to short excerpts of each movement listed in Figure 3.2 and describe how (or whether) Rameau creates musical

Representational Tropes in Text, Image, and Music 51

Real	Fanfarinette (musical) La Poule (animal) Les Sauvages (ethnographic; dance)
Idealized	Les Tricotets (dance) Les Triolets (literature) L'Egiptienne (ethnographic; gendered)
Fictional	La Triomphante (gendered) L'Indifferente (gendered)
Conceptual	Les Trois Mains (technical) L'Enharmonique (theoretical)

Figure 3.2 **Rameau's *Nouvelles Suites* (1726–27)**. Character pieces, organized by how their titles convey musical mimesis.

mimesis. Make comparisons between the musical styles, demands, and gestures among and between the individual movements and their representational categories. Discuss dance meters and binary forms. Consider the musical and bodily rhetoric created through performance. Open the lecture to more interactive segments; introduce new concepts before each new segment, followed by discussion and in-class analysis. Use "think-pair-share" models to keep the pace moving forward.

Discussion and Analysis

- Have students compare how the categories "real," "idealized," "fictional," and "conceptual" map onto the "Mimesis and Mockery" framework shown in Figure 3.1. What is the difference between the "real" (i.e., the things, people, and sounds that exist) and how Rameau fictionalized them through music? What does the music of "Les Sauvages" tell us about how Rameau perceived American Indian musics and dance traditions? For example, how does he "translate" what he heard (meaning, what he was *able* to hear and how he interpreted it) into French baroque forms and gestures that would be recognizable to his audiences? How do ethnic stereotypes emerge through musical translation? For example, what does it mean about Rameau's hearing and listening practices that he used a repetitive form with limited harmonic and melodic range? What are the challenges with "translation" in other ethnographic or primary sources?

- Discuss the collection as a musical "cabinet of curiosities," showing images and descriptions of who collected such cabinets, which objects they normally held, how they were displayed, how they participated in a baroque culture of "wonder" (*meraviglia*), and how they became precursors to natural history museums.[5]
- Return to Figure 3.2 from this perspective, considering how Rameau created a musical "cabinet of curiosities" through different layers of representation: 1) *real* (actual musical sounds, an animal, and real peoples and events, i.e., the danced demonstration by American Indians that Rameau witnessed); 2) *idealized* (things that exist in reality but do not have sounds associated with them, i.e., a poetic genre, a dance type, and an imagined person); 3) *fictional* (i.e., women not identified, and possibly not real, but embodying an emotion, character, or state of being); and 4) *conceptual* (i.e., an abstract idea, referencing a performative, technical, or theoretical challenge).
- As a collection of "curiosities," what does it mean that two "othered" ethnic groups are represented (an Egyptian woman and a group of American Indian peoples) in the musical books? What does it mean that all the representations of people are either ethnographic or gendered female? Where would you place these ethnographic and gendered representations on the scale of "invisibility/hypervisibility" and "mimesis/mockery" from Figure 3.2? What does it mean to "possess" culture through the act of collecting?

Provide greater context about the term "sauvages," highlighting the differences between modern usage (wild, unspoiled, i.e.,: wild animals, wilderness; unsociable; savage, ferocious, fierce; unauthorized, unofficial) and seventeenth-century usage (savage, brute, primitive). For advanced graduate classes, have students find eighteenth-century primary sources from a variety of linguistic or disciplinary contexts, and consider what bearing those usages bring to Rameau's representation in the *Nouvelles Suites*.

After students have analyzed these various levels of representation in Rameau's keyboard suites, they are ready to interpret how the expanded version of "Les Sauvages" works within the opéra-ballet *Les Indes galantes* (Entrée IV, 1736). The stage version brings new layers of meaning through text, image, and dance. Students should become familiar with French baroque operatic and dance conventions before embarking on this next step. (Box 3.4.)

> **Box 3.4: Lecture Idea—Baroque Drama and Identity**
>
> A unit on French baroque opera and drama should have at least one class day devoted to staged dance in its various forms, including *ballet de cour*, *tragédie en musique*, and *opéra-ballet*. The *entrée* and the *divertissement* were important structural factors in the development of these genres, and in the audience's perception of the plot. Today, in our fast-paced film and media environment, students may overlook these contained moments as "fluff" and scroll past them to get to the narrative. Rather, these moments provided an important sense of "repose," giving the audience a chance to contemplate the complicated plot intrigues. They function much like the Greek chorus in ancient tragedy.
>
> They also delineate cultural rituals (religious rites, marriages, war, or death) or can hasten the plot towards a dramatic moment (sleep scenes and storm scenes). These are moments where social hierarchies are made plain, and where characters from different stations in life can interact (gods, goddesses, nobles, shepherds, soldiers, peasants) and where ethnized characters are "othered." The combination of social hierarchy and ethnic othering can elicit in-class discussion of how these works interacted with political regimes and colonization. (See bibliography for helpful readings about blackface, historical performance practices, and empire.)

One of the most common "apologies" for the representation of Indigenous Americans in "Les Sauvages" is the comic or satirical tone of the work. Although this tone comes through in the various modern staged productions, the original text itself is *not* "comic." It is only "comic" in the early modern sense that there is no tragedy implied in the plot, and it has a happy ending. It is also not a "parody" or "satire." There are some implied jabs at the French and Spanish colonists who compete for the American Indian princess Zima's hand in marriage—but mostly the work consists of stock character types and pastoral scenic conventions.

To distinguish between the original text and our performance conventions, assign students to read selections of the *livret*/libretto, and analyze the representation of each character before viewing the same excerpt(s) in class and discussing the differences between the original text and the performed version. Prior to the initial assignment, students should be made aware of the French Jesuit strategies to Christianize and assimilate Indigenous peoples into French cultural norms through missionary work, agricultural and educational training, and even marriage. How are these values and practices represented in the text?

Students should also become aware of the "noble savage" idea that emerged in eighteenth-century French culture; using the "Mimesis to Mockery" framework, discuss how this idea functions as a "minimizing" strategy. This may seem counterintuitive to some students, who may wonder, "How can idealizing a culture be harmful?" The "Mimesis to Mockery" framework helps students to see that "misrepresentation" falls under the "mockery" paradigm. If Indigenous American cultures were truly "revered"—then why have so many historical inequities occurred (land access and preservation, education, health outcomes, extraction of cultural resources, etc.)? Students need to understand the lack of logic at work here. Misrepresentation leads to hypervisibility; hypervisibility enables deleterious actions. In the case of American Indian peoples, the result has been to make their cultures and presence less visible to everyday society and enables people from outside the community to control how they are represented in various media.

Assignment

Have students read excerpts from the text, answering some or all of the following questions:

1. How are the Indigenous characters—Zima and Adario—portrayed?
   a) What themes or stereotypes emerge from the text?
2. What does it mean that mythological, classical, and pastoral imagery from the ancient Greek and Roman literary tradition is overlaid onto real, contemporary cultures belonging to Indigenous peoples?
3. How are the French and Spanish colonists—Damon and Don Alvar—portrayed?
   a) What stereotypes or additional themes emerge from the text?
4. For each character, use the "mimesis to mockery" scale in Figure 3.1; how do the textual representations differ among characters?
5. How do the dynamics of colonialism and power alter the analytical results of the representation on the scale in Figure 3.1? How does knowledge of these practices change students' interpretations?
6. Given the colonial structure, how might we reinterpret the themes of "nature," "land," and "borders/shores" present throughout the entrée? What about ideals such as "beauty," "morality," and "love"?
7. How do musical forms and gestures add to the portrayals?

In-Class Discussion

- Begin with reviewing answers to the previously assigned questions in small groups, focusing on the results from the "mimesis to mockery" scale at each step, and then share with the full class. (The instructor should carefully monitor this process by interacting with each group.)
- How did each group revise their interpretations after considering colonial structures—or after discussing with classmates? Keep the focus of the discussion on the "Mimesis to Mockery" framework, having students justify their responses by quoting specific sections of the *livret*/libretto.
- After the full group discussion, students are now prepared to interact with video excerpts of the work. Then, students should answer a selection of the same questions they addressed for homework, focusing on how the performance changed their perception of each character, and why.

Only by following this sequence will students be able to make distinctions between the seventeenth-century work and our modern performance conventions.

Instructors must be very intentional about which production(s) they choose to show in class, and how they prepare students for discussion. Some productions exaggerate stereotypical depictions, while others transfer the identity-based concepts onto completely different social issues (such as environmentalism, post-war realities, or modern street culture). It could be helpful to compare excerpts from different productions, their interpretations of identity, and how their choices impact the audience's relationship to the text. Before initiating discussion, it is important to remind students of the classroom policies regarding respectful dialogue.

Instructors must also prepare themselves for the widely varying responses that students may have in the classroom and be clear on how they intend to respond. I recommend that students have a copy of the "mimesis to mockery" scale as a handout while watching the production(s) together in the classroom and that they have an opportunity to discuss their ideas in small groups with instructor supervision before any ideas are shared with the whole group; this may work best with a smaller class and with more advanced students. Alternatively, this discussion activity could be converted into an at-home assignment with a brief written response, so that instructors can review comments before sharing specific viewpoints with the full group; this approach is especially recommended for large lecture classes or for introductory and intermediate undergraduate students.

After this in-depth analysis, instructors should guide students in a discussion about the history of how this work ended up in the canon of French baroque opera. Why is it so popular today? Why is it more popular than other works by Rameau that are rarely performed? As discussed in William Gibbons' book, *Building the Operatic Museum*,[6] the canon of what we now call French baroque opera was created by a small group of famous musicians at the turn of the twentieth century, who made editions and created performances to highlight French nationality and history. Their goal was to create a cultural "museum;" this idea should resonate with the previous classroom discussion of the "cabinet of curiosities" regarding Rameau's keyboard collection. *Les Sauvages* was included in this project as part of a "museum collection" establishing a canon of French baroque opera alongside works with classical mythological subjects treated as tragedies. While the works based on mythology would have established France as an inheritor of ancient Greek and Roman (i.e., "Western") culture, *Les Sauvages* would define "Frenchness" from a perspective of colonialism. *Les Sauvages* creates an operatic perspective of a culture that was distinctly "not French" (i.e., Indigenous), but portrayed according to French conventions, idioms, and belief systems.

The resulting portrayal included the use of blackface onstage in both the original 1736 version,[7] and in productions such as the opera-ballet's first modern revival in 1952 in Paris, under the direction of Maurice Lehmann. While many may have the notion that blackface was (and is) not considered offensive in Europe, this genre was just as prevalent as a form of racist portrayal as in the U.S. In addition to the blackface practices that were already present in early modern France,[8] American style blackface minstrelsy was exported to Europe in the nineteenth century, commercialized, and disseminated in many forms. Primary sources indicate that it was understood as a demeaning portrayal. For the most advanced students (such as in a graduate seminar), instructors might consider visual comparisons between the costuming in William Christie's production (especially during the "Les Sauvages" *divertissement*) and blackface images from minstrelsy. For suitable examples to use in the classroom (only if the instructor deems the students mature enough to do so respectfully), see the website of the Jim Crow Museum of Racist Memorabilia.[9]

Students should consider the following questions: When is historical "authenticity" harmful? At what point should we reinterpret or rewrite historical stage dramas? How can we perform this work ethically today? Should we perform this work at all? If so, under what conditions?

Creating Positive Musical Images

While Case Study 6 focuses on historical representation of an "othered" identity, Cases Studies 7 and 8 explore how composers created new representations that fought back against old tropes. The composer Florence Price

(1887–1953) and the innovative blues musician Muddy Waters (McKinley Morganfield, 1913–1983) both used music to reframe identity. Both artists were working in Chicago, after participating in the Great Migration, in an era that was bounded on one side by the Harlem Renaissance and on the other side by the Civil Rights Movement. (See Chapter 5 for more on this era of African-American musical creativity.) These case studies demonstrate how the "Mimesis to Mockery" framework can be used to analyze representation of identity when the artist or originator depicts her or his own culture. Both musicians discussed here created bold new images that counteracted harmful stereotypes.

Like Scott Joplin's *Treemonisha* (Chapter 2, Case Study 5), and like other compositions influenced by the Harlem Renaissance movement, Price's *Dances in the Canebrakes* (1953) combines classical forms with Black folk idioms. Although Price has become more famous in the public sphere through scholarly reconstructions and new performances and recordings of her large-scale works, there is less scholarly attention on (and therefore fewer classroom resources for) her small-scale works. By contrast, Waters' "Mannish Boy" (1955) received a wider original circulation due to its popular distribution on record albums, influenced by the artist's fame and his reputation for having created an electric blues sound that contributed to the development of rock and roll. However, his music is less likely to be included in traditional music history curricula, even as blues, jazz, electronic, and popular musics continue to receive greater focus.

To use the "Mimesis to Mockery" framework to analyze both *Dances in the Canebrakes* and "Mannish Boy" requires advanced critical skills. Compared to Rameau's "Les Sauvages" (Case Study 6), musical images are not immediately evident in the performance of the respective works; rather, they need to be uncovered. In this respect, the process resembles identifying the shadow history of the work—we are locating the sometimes-unspoken symbolism that indicates the artist's ability to speak differently to different audiences. (See Chapter 5 on the concept of signifying.) The hidden symbolism becomes evident when we rely on interdisciplinary and intertextual sources. To do this work, scholars and instructors must identify external sources of imagery or imagistic language representing social norms and political customs, based on historical and current events, literature, newspapers, and other primary sources—or deriving from other musical genres ranging from minstrelsy to musical theater and film—to build an interpretation.

Case Study 7: Florence Price, *Dances in the Canebrakes* (1953)

Price's piano suite *Dances in the Canebrakes* merges the traditional keyboard dance suite with vernacular musical gestures that might evoke scenarios familiar to the composer's Southern upbringing in Arkansas. The three movements create an overarching narrative cycle: I. "Nimble Feet," II. "Tropical Noon," and III. "Silk Hat and Walking Cane." While the first and last movements use syncopation to illustrate a congruity between music and dance implied in the titles, the middle movement invokes rest during the heat of the day. While movements one and two have titles that are quite straightforward, movement three is somewhat perplexing. What do the "Silk Hat" and the "Walking Cane" represent? Proud Sunday church finery? Folk African-American cakewalk dancing? Minstrelsy? Business attire?

The answer depends entirely on how we situate the time and place of the scenario. In the South, proud Sunday church finery would most likely apply to post-Emancipation eras. Folk cakewalk dancing would imply Southern practices associated with slavery. Minstrelsy would represent a perversion of Black musical practices and emerging musical theater, and could be located at any time from the late nineteenth century up to Price's own day, depending on the genre and medium of the depiction. Likewise, business attire could imply any of these eras, contingent on location.

Price's title to the suite (*Dances in the Canebrakes*) suggests an authentic, folk rendering in a protected outdoor space. Canebrakes are tall bamboo stands native to Southern swampy regions in the U.S., of which few are left today; in the nineteenth century, these were places that could protect runaway slaves. In Price's composition, the musical reminiscences together with the titular imagery can recall multiple signifiers simultaneously.[10] (See Box 3.5.)

Box 3.5: Research Project—Analyzing Image, Text, and Music

To develop independent research skills for students at all levels, it is important to first offer a framework, methodology, or process to follow. This exercise pairs well with the skills explored in Box 3.2 on interpreting dance gestures in Jacquet de la Guerre's keyboard suites. Now that students are familiar with the "Mimesis to Mockery" framework, have them use it as an analytical tool in their own individual or group research projects.

After reflecting on the various meanings of the titles in Price's keyboard suite *Dances in the Canebrakes*, have students work on an individual assignment or collaborative research project to build an "archive" of visual and textual connotations from the early twentieth century to the present, demonstrating how those key words or topics appeared in various media. Where does each representation fall on the "mimesis to mockery" spectrum? What were the debates, conflicts, or commonalities between the various representations involved? How might Price have responded to those through music? How did other artists of her era—or since—respond to similar texts and images? Each student should contribute one historical item with analytical commentary that also considers how Price and other artists used reversals (such as "signifying," "masking," and "double consciousness," discussed in Chapter 5) to undo harmful stereotypes.

The third movement of Price's *Dances in the Canebrakes* takes the place of a typical "allegro" movement in sonata form, which Price frequently fulfills using the syncopated, lively, jaunty, and up-tempo gestures of the traditional African-American "juba dance." Exploring the various meanings of the word "juba," from an African dance to the term's appropriation in minstrelsy, and everything in between, brings new interpretations to Price's "Silk Hat and Walking Cane." (Box 3.6.)

Box 3.6: Lecture Idea; Envisioning the "Juba"

Instructors may wish to show videos of traditional African-American folk dance and body percussion related to the "juba dance," such as patting juba, the ring shout, the cakewalk, and the hambone, each of which also has its own derivatives. Several examples are freely available online; just ensure that the performer is well qualified in the tradition, to avoid showing appropriative or exoticizing examples. (Professor Julia Grella O'Connell has made several good videos available on her course website: https://oconnellmusic101.com/2018/09/18/juba/; the Geechee Gullah Ring Shouters and the McIntosh County Shouters also have online videos available.) To emphasize the "Mimesis to Mockery" framework, instructors may wish to show some examples of how the "juba dance" was represented in sheet music as part of the minstrelsy tradition—and, by contrast, images of the famous African-American dancer William Henry Lane, whose stage name was Master Juba.

The name and the dance tradition "juba" came from slaves brought from the Congo to Charleston, S.C.; later, white Americans called this dance the "Charleston" and it became a hugely popular dance craze. The word "juba" (meaning to beat time rhythmically in Bantu) should not be confused with Juba, the city in South Sudan, which was also a major slave market for the Muslim/Eastern slave trade.

60 Representational Tropes in Text, Image, and Music

As a musical theater construct (performed authentically by African Americans), the juba dance also merged with several Euro-American traditions, such as reels, jigs, and clog dancing, and adopted musical aspects from ragtime. In strictly musical terms, Price's references to the juba in her orchestrated compositions makes certain these connections are especially clear, such as in the third movement of the *Symphony in E Minor* (which is titled "Juba").

However much we make these modern comparisons, our understanding and appreciation of past folk tradition is necessarily oversimplified; as outsiders, from a modern perspective, we will never be able to achieve accurate historical understanding of either the original African cultures or their retentions and amalgamations in the nineteenth-century Americas—nor how they morphed and changed over time to become uniquely American.

In symbolic terms, the juba style in Price's "Silk Hat and Walking Cane" refers to all these past lineages. By articulating a slower, moderate tempo with lyrical, sweeping melodic gestures paired with chromatic harmonic inflections and a less active bassline, the composer transforms the theatrical costume of the juba or cakewalk (whether associated with African-American musical theater or its demeaning depiction in minstrelsy) into a new, more dignified portrayal of Black male identity. Price simultaneously restores associations such as church finery or business attire to this imagery, or upscale ballroom dance traditions, while invoking the "New Negro" aesthetic of the Harlem Renaissance. Price thus uses music as resistance, overturning sonic associations with minstrelsy characters such as "Juba" and "Zip Coon" to convey a sophisticated, urbane Black male body. (Box 3.7.)

Box 3.7: Research Project—Working with "Archives"

For beginning and intermediate students, instructors may wish to assign an "archive" of related primary sources. Advanced students can accomplish an archival project using collections held by their institutional library, or by the local public library. Working together with archival librarians to structure a course unit based on related materials (personal papers, letters, concert programs, film, posters, recordings, radio broadcasts, etc.), holding class sessions in the archive, and requiring students to complete certain research tasks or a set number of hours in the library, are all great ways of bringing the process to life for advanced undergraduate and graduate students.

An archival project of this nature can also be conducted in a collaborative effort. Consider alternative formats for the final project. Blogs, vlogs, student-conducted interviews, podcasts, or digital visualization tools such as timelines or network graphs are all formats that allow students to "show their work" (i.e., what processes or analysis led to their final interpretation?) and to incorporate multi-media sources involving image, text, and music with visually engaging results. It is best if students do not focus on biographical details about the composer/artist's life but bring original analytical interpretations back to the musical work at hand. This way they avoid simply duplicating summaries of already-published material.

Florence Price and Teaching Strategies

Although my focus here is on Price's piano suite *Dances with the Canebrakes*, instructors will probably also want to teach at least one of Price's works for larger ensembles, such as the *Symphony in E Minor* (1932) or the *Piano Concerto in One Movement* (1934). The *Symphony* marks a historic moment in African-American music, as the first by a Black woman to be played by a major orchestra; it won first prize in the Wanamaker Competition in 1932, was premiered by the Chicago Symphony in 1933, and was repeated at the Chicago World's Fair later the same year. The *Piano Concerto* was also performed by the Women's Symphony Orchestra of Chicago in 1934, and later by the Chicago Symphony. These large-scale works demonstrate Price's skill at orchestration, and use of classical form and harmony, blended with African-American idioms.

In-Class Listening Exercise

Step 1. Have students listen to excerpts from each of the movements of the *Symphony in E Minor*, while posing the following scenario:

You are a concert reviewer or music historian asked to describe an unknown work to a public audience. Which musical gestures, styles, and influences do you hear in Florence Price's *Symphony in E minor*?

Have students take notes while listening, using general terms from music theory as much as possible. Between each movement, have students share (quickly) their results to the whole class (or in small groups); keep a list of terms on the board, and discuss.

Step 2. As a follow-up activity, have students write a brief "concert review" or "scholarly analysis" (one paragraph) of the *Symphony*, using the list of terms from the board.

> Advanced students can compare the terminology used in publications from a variety of sources and time periods (newspapers, websites, scholarship), including primary source reviews of the original 1953 performance.[11]
> Have students compare these published descriptions to their own, addressing the following questions:
>
> > Are there ways that we can improve our communication about music by African-American composers? How do concert reviews potentially impact the acceptance of a work into the classical canon? How does scholarship impact our desire to listen to, study, or perform unfamiliar works—or shape our listening experiences?
>
> **Step 3** (or an alternative to Step 2). Have students compare the use of African-American materials in Price's *Symphony in E Minor* and in William Grant Still's *Afro-American Symphony* (1930).

One of the challenges with teaching African-American music, is that students may have an incomplete understanding of how social and political factors are directly correlated with composers' biographies, and how those intertwining circumstances impact musical composition and reception histories. In my teaching, I ensure that students are aware of the major political movements that intersect with African-American lives and livelihoods in conjunction with teaching the repertory. Students are often surprised that an initial Civil Rights Act was proposed as early as 1875, and that African-American "Freedmen" had the right to vote in the South, but these rights were curtailed and denied by local laws and customs. Students are also surprised that the Great Migration continued past the early twentieth century into the 1970s. (See Box 3.8.)

Price was born just ten years after Reconstruction ended in 1877; after this date, the legal protection of civil rights for African Americans in the South were no longer guaranteed (until the Civil Rights Act of 1964). Price's early life was therefore marked by Jim Crow laws put into effect from the 1870s through 1880s.

During this time, segregation was widespread, according to two types of conventions: legal (*de jure*) and social (*de facto*). Southern states enacted laws (*de jure*) that enforced segregation and reduced civil rights for African Americans; those living in the North faced similar restrictions by social convention (*de facto*), backed by personal or institutional intimidation. The Plessy v. Ferguson decision at the Supreme Court (1896) legally enforced segregation at the federal level, making life more difficult for Black communities everywhere in the U.S.

Box 3.8: Lecture Idea—Florence Price and a Timeline of African-American History

Here is an example of a timeline that I discuss with my students in my African-American Music class:
1865–1877: **Reconstruction**—enacted civil rights to ensure freedoms of ex-slaves

Jim Crow Laws

- 1870s–1880s: Southern States enacted laws to enforce racial segregation (*de jure*); similar practices occurred in other areas, without legislation (*de facto*)
- 1896: Such laws were upheld at the federal level in the Supreme Court case Plessy v. Ferguson (public facilities can be "separate but equal")

Civil Rights Movement

- 1875: First "Civil Rights Act" introduced
- Renewed efforts again after World War II
- Civil Rights (1965) and Voting Rights Act (1966)

To demonstrate the initial successes of the Reconstruction period, I included an image of a print titled "Freedmen Vote in New Orleans" dated 1867.[12] These freedoms, of course, came at great cost—not only the enormous cost of the Civil War, which ended in 1865, but also the cost of lives and property in the race-based violence of the New Orleans Massacre of 1866, and the earlier Memphis Riots of 1866. This spurred political action towards the Fourteenth Amendment in 1868, which granted African-Americans rights to citizenship, and the Fifteenth Amendment in 1870, which protected the right to vote (although there were still local laws and customs such as "grandfather clauses" and poll taxes that excluded African Americans).

Price's family lived through racial violence in Arkansas; Jim Crow laws limited her father's ability to maintain his dental practice, causing a downturn in their financial status. Once a successful, well-off medical practitioner, he died leaving a substantial amount of debt.[13]

Facing lack of opportunities, and dealing with turbulent and threatening racial violence, Price joined the Great Migration twice; first, by attending the New England Conservatory in Boston, and second by moving to Chicago after leaving her first teaching position at Clark Atlanta University. The financial loss and social uprooting created by the systemic racism experienced by Price and her family (and by many like her) cannot be overestimated. Born to a family of successful professionals who hosted sophisticated intellectuals and musicians in their home, Price struggled financially despite her recognition and success as a composer and performer; she ended her career living in a residence home for artists, writers, and musicians in Chicago, where she taught piano. Students should understand that the racist legal, social, and educational systems in the U.S. not only prevented African Americans from reaching their full potential in life, but also caused instability, financial insecurity, and degrading circumstances for those who had worked hard to make successful lives for themselves, compounding the impact on future generations.

Despite these serious and life-changing setbacks, African-American composers and artists used music and material arts to overturn stereotypes and reinforce positive images for contemporary audiences, especially in reaction to discrimination or violence. Art exhibits and exhibition catalogues, exhibit reviews in newspapers and magazines, and scholarship on related artists are prime starting points for information. (See Chapter 5.) Ask students to reflect on modern equivalences. How do clothing and appearance accumulate political and moral associations today? How have these become sources of discrimination or protest? How have artists reframed and reformulated such images using media other than music? What is the role of classical and popular musics in changing societal perceptions?

Segregation and discrimination have also had an impact on our scholarly pathways. Much of the published materials on American symphonies and symphonic composers remains to be reintegrated with the works of African-American and women composers. Why does scholarship about George Whitefield Chadwick not discuss Price alongside his other famous students? And why does scholarship on Edgard Varèse not include William Grant Still, while mentioning his other famous students? These are glaring omissions in historiography. The classroom is a valuable place to address these inequities; class discussions and collaborative research projects can fill in the historiographical gaps and spur critical thinking about how we define "American music." (See Boxes 3.9, 3.10, 3.11.) Advanced students looking for honors thesis, master's thesis, or dissertation topics might consider approaches that explore portions of these histories, and researchers might consider revising the overarching narratives involving these composers. (See also Chapter 1, Case Study 2.)

Box 3.9: Syllabus Design—Florence Price and Early African-American Symphonic Music

Design a module on early African-American symphonic music to contextualize Florence Price, including the composers William Grant Still (1895–1978) and William Dawson (1899–1990). To fully appreciate the musical style of these works, students should be well-versed in the Negro spiritual first; arrangements of spirituals by Harry T. Burleigh (1866–1949) would provide a solid background. (See also Chapter 2, Case Study 5.)

Box 3.10: Syllabus Design—Florence Price and Women as Early Orchestral Composers in the U.S.

Create a module studying early compositions for orchestra by American women, such as Amy Marcy Cheney Beach (1867–1944), Marion Eugénie Bauer (1882–1955), and Louise Juliette Talma (1906–1996). Denise Von Glahn's book titled *Music and the Skillful Listener* includes chapters on all three composers. Assignments from this book can lead to discussions about the dichotomy between long-held stereotypes associating women with the natural world, and the expanding ability for women to explore the physical world and its natural settings in the early twentieth century. How did Florence Price's education, life, career, and compositional focus differ from the women discussed in Von Glahn's book?

Box 3.11: Syllabus Design/Collaborative Research Project—Florence Price and Traditional Historiography

Construct a linear history of major influences in American music, focusing on the students of Price's teacher, George Whitefield Chadwick (1854–1931). A short list might include works by: Horatio William Parker (1863–1919); Margaret Ruthven Lang (1867–1972); Frederick Shepherd Converse (1871–1940), who also taught Florence Price; and Mabel Wheeler Daniels (1878–1971). These composers all have works recorded by major orchestras and other prominent artists. This module could explore the impact of the Second New England

School on the subsequent generation, considering what makes music "American," how composers represent place in music, why certain composers remain in the performance canon while others lose popularity over time, or how original concert reviews impact a composer's staying power in the repertory.

A fruitful collaborative class research topic would be exploring scholarship on American musical nationalism in the twentieth century. Which sources include Florence Price? Students could answer this question via a collaborative library "scavenger hunt," adapted to different levels as a "getting-to-know the library" assignment and to develop research and topic framing skills.

Case Study 8: Muddy Waters, "Mannish Boy" (1955)

Muddy Waters began his career in the Mississippi Delta region; he was raised, and later worked as a sharecropper, on the Stovall Plantation, a large cotton farm near Clarksdale, where he played folk blues in the area. In 1941, ethnomusicologist/folklorist Alan Lomax (1915–2002) recorded the guitarist singing and playing acoustic blues, with interspersed interviews. Although most blues scholarship foregrounds Lomax, he worked collaboratively with Black professors from Fisk University (including composer/conductor John W. Work III, 1901–1967; and sociologist Dr. Charles S. Johnson, 1893–1956) to record a wide range of musical practices in Clarksdale, from religious hollers to folksongs and girls' games. The project resulted in archives held at Fisk University and the Archive of American Folk-Song at the Library of Congress.

These early acoustic songs recorded by Waters later became commercial hits after he moved to Chicago, where he founded the electric blues style. "Country Blues" (1941) brought him fame as the revised "I Feel Like Going Home" (1948), while "I Be's Troubled" (1941) became the hit "I Can't Be Satisfied" (1948), later covered by the Rolling Stones in 1965. Waters' hard driving electric slide guitar, provocative lyrics, and innovative instrumentation influenced the development of rock and roll; the Rolling Stones, the Beatles, Eric Clapton, and other rock artists named Waters as a significant influence on their sound. (Box 3.12.)

Box 3.12: Class Activity, Listening Exercise—Musical and Textual Interpretation of the Blues

Listen to Robert Johnson 1911–1938), "Walking Blues" (1936). Have students identify common blues themes (blues chords, declamatory melodic cells, textual form, references to movement/migration, loss, blues feeling, relationships). The phrase "ride a blind" refers to hopping on the baggage car of a train, which has no windows—thus removing the rider's ability to see out. "Elgin movement" refers to the internal mechanisms of the Elgin wristwatch, guaranteed to be precise. How does the song reference current social and political events, such as the Great Depression and the Great Migration?

Listen to Muddy Waters, "I Feel Like Going Home" (1948)—a variation of his "Country Blues" (1941). Have students discuss the process of blues composition from the perspective of creative musical borrowing. (If time permits, discuss Muddy Waters' own compositional process by comparing the two different versions of his song.) Which musical and textual elements does Muddy Waters borrow from Johnson? How does Muddy Waters alter the song, using new musical and textual layers? How might "Feel Like Going Home" be interpreted as a trickster narrative, or as "signifying" using reversals, displacement, masking, irony, troping, or double speak? (One possible response: While in Johnson's song the blues brings on restlessness and a desire for travel, Waters' song invokes the weariness of the traveler and a desire to return home, thus inverting the typical paradigm of the wandering blues musician invoked in so many songs about travel.) How might Muddy Waters' rendition mark the nostalgia and loss of idealism sometimes expressed by Harlem Renaissance artists? (See Chapter 5 on signifying and the Harlem Renaissance.)

Compare the sentiments in Muddy Waters' "Feel Like Going Home" with Langston Hughes' poem "Red Clay Blues" (1939).

Waters transformed blues music not only through his new electric sound, but also through lyrics about love, sex, and identity. While relationships were always traditional themes in folk blues, they were often treated in a haphazard way, interspersed with other topics, and articulated through euphemisms, double speak, or signifying. (See Chapter 5.) By contrast, Waters delivers strong narrative self-projection. From his first commercial recording after arriving in Chicago—with the lyrics "You know the Gypsy woman told me / That you your mother's bad luck child," in "Gypsy Woman" (1947)—he cultivates strong authorial control, creating identity dualities between past and present.[14] The most famous songs, which influenced the rock revolution, demand attention to authorial identity, as in "Rollin' Stone" (1950), "Hoochie Coochie Man" (1954), and "Got My Mojo Working" (1957).

"Mannish Boy" (1955) fits this paradigm and offers several interpretive possibilities. Loudly proclaiming identity as a "M-A-N" asserts civil rights in the face of demeaning social practices, while boasting sexual prowess. The insistent repetition of one chord, the percussive rhythm, and the scoop up to a higher vocal pitch on the word "man"—reversing the typical blues melodic formulas—intensify the meaning. The text drives the music, perhaps more so than in any other Waters song. Although he recorded this song in May of 1955, by the end of summer it may have accumulated new meanings for audiences. In August, Emmet Till, a fourteen-year-old boy from Chicago, traveled to Mississippi with relatives, where he was kidnapped and murdered. By September, the primary Black newspaper in Chicago was elevating awareness of this case by writing to President Dwight D. Eisenhower, asking whether he planned to "take any action with respect to this shocking act of lawlessness."[15] Till's open casket funeral is considered a turning point in the civil rights movement; this horrific event dominated Chicago media, likely causing audiences to re-orient themselves around music lyrics such as "Mannish Boy."

Although scholarship on the Harlem Renaissance is mostly silent about the blues (preferring instead to discuss jazz), I argue that this genre was motivated by the same issues: the Great Migration, political activism, and re-casting folk traditions into new forms. If—as so many scholars have asserted—the blues could serve as a foundation, a metaphor, a process emulated by fine arts and art music—then why should we exclude the blues from Harlem Renaissance scholarship? (Box 3.13.) Historically, this exclusion occurred since the blues did not qualify as social "uplift" in early twentieth-century aesthetics; popular music was not elite enough and did not represent the educational goals set forth by W.E.B. DuBois and others. Jazz was already marginal in this regard.

> **Box 3.13: Class Discussion—Music and Racial Politics**
>
> What is a "mannish boy"? Why would Muddy Waters feel the need to proclaim his status as a "man"? What was happening politically in the 1950s?
> How did the Great Migration impact both Florence Price and Muddy Waters? How did each artist respond differently to the aesthetics of the Harlem Renaissance/Chicago Black Renaissance?

If we truly embrace African-American literary and musical aesthetics from this time period, we cannot allow the blues origin myth/shadow history framing to remain. We must understand that Price and Waters participated in the same project, at the same time, in the same city—using different musical means. Both artists, especially evident in *Dances in the Canebrakes* and "Mannish Boy," created new images of the Black male body, advocating for equality and respect.

Notes

1 See my article, "Race and Representation in Baroque Opera—Some Thoughts on Pedagogy, Scholarship, and Performance," in the journal *Historical Performance* Vol. 3 (2020).
2 For background on this field of study and its key terminology, see: Richard Delgado and Jean Stefancic, *Critical Race Theory: The Cutting Edge*, 2013, http://site.ebrary.com/id/10754199; Richard Delgado and Jean Stefancic, *Critical Race Theory: An Introduction*, Third edition (New York: New York University Press, 2017); Marvin Lynn and Adrienne D. Dixson, eds., *Handbook of Critical Race Theory in Education*, Second edition (New York, NY: Routledge, 2021), https://doi.org/10.4324/9781351032223.
3 For an informative and accessible presentation on this theme, see Patricia Ann Neely, "A Circle of Fifths: A Retrospective and Remedy for Addressing Diversity in Early Music in America," https://www.youtube.com/watch?v=RQErcLesP1g.
4 The 1935 performance of *Les Indes galantes* included only three entrées: *Le Turc généreux* (The Generous Turk), *Les Incas du Pérou* (The Incas of Peru), and *Les Fleurs* (The Flowers), which is set in a Persian flower garden. The fourth entrée, *Les Sauvages* was added in 1736.
5 Paula Findlen, *Possessing Nature: Museums, Collecting, and Scientific Culture in Early Modern Italy*, 1. paperback printing, [Nachdr.], Studies on the History of Society and Culture 20 (Berkeley: Univ. of California Press, 2010), https://doi.org/10.1525/9780520917781.
6 William Gibbons, *Building the Operatic Museum: Eighteenth-Century Opera in Fin-de-Siecle Paris*, vol. 99, Eastman Studies in Music (Rochester: University of Rochester Press, 2013).
7 Olivia Bloechl, "Race, Empire, and Early Music," in *Rethinking Difference in Music Scholarship*, ed. Olivia Bloechl, Melanie Lowe, and Jeffrey Kallberg (Cambridge: Cambridge University Press, 2015), 77–107, https://doi.org/10.1017/CBO9781139208451.003.
8 Noémie Ndiaye, "Rewriting the *Grand Siècle*: Blackface in Early Modern France and the Historiography of Race," *Literature Compass* 18, no. 10 (2021), https://doi.org/10.1111/lic3.12603.
9 "The Origins of Jim Crow," Jim Crow Museum of Racist Memorabilia, Ferris State University, accessed April 26, 2019, https://www.ferris.edu/HTMLS/news/jimcrow/origins.htm.
10 My initial work on this topic was funded by the "Global Popular Music Initiative" in 2020–2021 on the theme of "Musical Bodies," hosted by Indiana University's "Platform: An Arts and Humanities Research Laboratory" with funding from the Andrew W. Mellon Foundation. This project resulted in a collaborative lecture recital titled "Born This Way: Black Bodies and Black Voices" with tenor Dr. Elektra Voyante, pianist Prof. Kimberly Carballo, and research assistant Jacqueline Fortier. This funding also resulted in a working paper titled "Popular Music and the Black Male Body."
11 Brown and Ramsey, *The Heart of a Woman*, 117–25, and Lawrence Schenbeck, "Music, Gender, and 'Uplift' in the 'Chicago Defender,' 1927–1937," *The Musical Quarterly* 81, no. 3 (1997): 344–70.
12 available at the New York Public Library Digital Collections; https://digitalcollections.nypl.org/items/510d47e1-3fd9-a3d9-e040-e00a18064a99.
13 Rae Linda Brown and Guthrie P. Ramsey, *The Heart of a Woman: The Life and Music of Florence B. Price*, Music in American Life (Urbana: University of Illinois Press, 2020), 72.

14 See Ayana Smith, "Blues, Criticism, and the Signifying Trickster," *Popular Music* 24, no. 2, Literature and Music (2005): 179–91, for discussion of the "signifying trickster" identity in the blues.

15 "Telegram, Chicago Defender to DDE Re: Emmett Till Case, September 1, 1995," September 1, 1955, DDE's Records as President, Alphabetical File, Box 3113, Emmett Till, Dwight D. Eisenhower Presidential Library, https://www.eisenhowerlibrary.gov/sites/default/files/research/online-documents/civil-rights-emmett-till-case/1955-09-01-chicago-defender-to-dde.pdf.

Annotated Bibliography

Critical Race Theory (CRT)

For instructors who wish to learn more about the tenets of CRT, I recommend the following sources:

Delgado, Richard, and Jean Stefancic. *Critical Race Theory: An Introduction.* Third edition. New York: New York University Press, 2017.

For the briefest of introductions to the subject, see section F ("Basic Tenets of Critical Race Theory") on pp. 8–11 of the Introduction; for a more detailed explanation, see Chapter II: "Hallmark Critical Race Theory Themes," pp. 19–43. Please note: the classroom exercises and discussion questions described in this book would not be appropriate for any humanities classroom, since they are intended for legal studies. Students in a music classroom would not have the case law background to answer these questions in a thoughtful way based on factual or historical evidence; using these prompts in a music classroom would simply be an invitation to politically motivated, personal, or religious "opinion" making that could cause negative classroom dynamics and be significantly harmful for marginalized students. I recommend this resource primarily for instructors wishing to gain some introductory background knowledge on the subject.

———. *Critical Race Theory: The Cutting Edge*, 2013. http://site.ebrary.com/id/10754199.

There are many good essays here with implications for race, culture, society, and law. For those interested in understanding how the social constructs of race are embedded into our society—and the resulting impacts on individuals—I recommend Ian F. Haney-Lopez' Chapter 24, "The Social Construction of Race" (pp. 238–48). This chapter demonstrates why it is important to study how the representation of race and other identities are embedded in cultural products (such as opera, musical theater, art, or other representational genres), and can provide instructors with ready answers to difficult topics or questions in class, such as: why do we have to study this? Or what does race have to do with music?

Ladson-Billings, Gloria, and William F. Tate, IV. "Toward a Critical Race Theory of Education." *Teachers College Record* 97, no. 1 (1995): 47–68.

This article is a seminal work that is frequently cited in the literature on CRT; it is a helpful background reading for students. It is a good strategy to assign this article as a reading at the beginning of a semester on African-American music or in other courses where race will be discussed. Students will be confronted with their own lack of knowledge on the historical factors discussed in this article; instructors will need to be prepared to have an open and honest response. As always, it is important to remind students of class policies on how to discuss sensitive topics in ethical ways; the key is always to ask questions instead of making declarative statements, and to avoid offensive language. When describing the assignment, review these policies with your students and direct them to any official institutional policies on hate speech and microaggressions; taken together, the assignment and the discussion parameters and policies will set your students up for a successful and respectful semester where everyone experiences learning growth.

Lynn, Marvin, and Adrienne D. Dixson, eds. *Handbook of Critical Race Theory in Education*. Second edition. New York, NY: Routledge, 2021. https://doi.org/10.4324/9781351032223.

For instructors and students in the field of music education, this is an important source. I especially recommend Joyce M. McCall's "Straight No Chaser: An Unsung Blues" (Chapter 15, pp. 203–20). Since most students that I encounter are woefully uneducated on the history of Black thought and intellectual traditions, I also highly recommend Reiland Rabaka's "W.E.B. DuBois's Contributions to Critical Race Studies in Education" (Chapter 5, pp. 62–78). For an introduction to the field, see Chapter 1, "The History and Conceptual Elements of Critical Race Theory," by Kevin Brown and Darrell D. Jackson (pp. 9–21).

Diversity in Early Music

Neely, Patricia Ann. "A Circle of Fifths: A Retrospective and Remedy for Addressing Diversity in Early Music in America." Presented for Early Music America, April 6, 2020. https://www.youtube.com/watch?v=RQErcLesP1g.

A highly informative overview of the pr®esence of diverse identities in early modern Europe. There are many more resources on diversity in early music; I encourage instructors to seek out topics on this subject, to include Europe, Asia, the Americas, and global music history.

Graham, Sandra J. *Spirituals and the Birth of a Black Entertainment Industry*. Music in American Life. Urbana: University of Illinois Press, 2018. https://doi.org/10.5622/illinois/9780252041631.001.0001.

A history of the African-American spiritual as a concert genre, beginning with the Fisk Jubilee Singers, and how the genre influenced American popular and commercial musics, including minstrelsy. The book also discusses how the spiritual was used to create a "Black identity" in the U.S.; readings from this book are appropriate for all levels, and are especially helpful paired with readings on critical race theory, or works representing Black identity onstage, such as Scott Joplin's *Treemonisha* or George Gershwin's *Porgy and Bess*. (Chapter 2, Case Study 5; Box 3.1)

Rameau and Les Sauvages

Bloechl, Olivia Ashley. *Native American Song at the Frontiers of Early Modern Music*. New Perspectives in Music History and Criticism 17. Cambridge: Cambridge University Press, 2020.

Traces the histories of how early colonists understood Native American singing practices, through to the representation of Indigenous peoples in staged music by Lully and Rameau.

72 *Representational Tropes in Text, Image, and Music*

Findlen, Paula. *Possessing Nature: Museums, Collecting, and Scientific Culture in Early Modern Italy*. Studies on the History of Society and Culture 20. Berkeley: University of California Press, 2010. https://doi.org/10.1525/9780520917781.

A fascinating history of the development of the modern museum from collecting practices. Discusses the items collected, where they came from, how they were obtained, how they were organized to create "sites of knowledge," and how they were used as the basis for early experimental practices leading to the era of the Enlightenment and the "new science." Read in conjunction with Bloechl, instructors can begin to frame the ideas of "sonic collections;" adding layers from scholarship on extractivism, we can start to create a theoretical frame for "sonic extractivism."

Jim Crow Museum of Racist Memorabilia, Ferris State University. "The Origins of Jim Crow." Accessed April 26, 2019. https://www.ferris.edu/HTMLS/news/jimcrow/origins.htm.

A useful website for identifying the various stereotypes arising from minstrelsy in the U.S.; instructors may wish to draw upon these for class discussions in situations where students have the maturity and intellectual ability to respond with seriousness, attentiveness, and sensitivity. The images can also be used for collaborative research projects. (Box 3.7.)

Pisani, Michael V. *Imagining Native America in Music*. New Haven, CT: Yale University Press, 2008. https://doi.org/10.12987/yale/9780300108934.001.0001.

The opening chapters discuss various ways in which stereotypes about American Indians were portrayed in baroque opera, court entertainments, theater, and song from the late sixteenth century through the early nineteenth century. The first chapter ("Noble Savagery in European Court Entertainments, 1550–1760," pp. 17–43) is most related to the context for Rameau's *Les Sauvages*.

Gibbons, William. *Building the Operatic Museum: Eighteenth-Century Opera in Fin-de-Siecle Paris*. Vol. 99, Eastman Studies in Music. Rochester: University of Rochester Press, 2013.

Provides a helpful perspective on canon building and nationalism; although this source does not discuss race, it can be helpful in understanding why certain works depicting "othered" groups were considered representative of French greatness in music.

Blackface in France

While this topic may not be suitable for discussion in every class, I encourage instructors to become knowledgeable on this subject so that they may answer any questions that arise regarding "authenticity" and performance practice in baroque music, or about the harmful history of using blackface in opera in both Europe and the U.S.:

Bloechl, Olivia Ashley, "Race, Empire, and Early Music." In *Rethinking Difference in Music Scholarship*, edited by Olivia Bloechl, Melanie Lowe, and Jeffrey Kallberg, 77–107. Cambridge: Cambridge University Press, 2015. https://doi.org/10.1017/CBO9781139208451.003.

Discusses costuming and blackface practices in works by Lully at the court of Louis XIV in the seventeenth century, and how these practices reflected political strategies of empire through performance.

Childs, Adrienne L., and Susan Houghton Libby, eds. *Blacks and Blackness in European Art of the Long Nineteenth Century*. First issued in paperback. London; New York: Routledge, Taylor & Francis Group, 2017.

Includes chapters on representations of blackness in late eighteenth-century Europe, and on blackface minstrelsy in France.

Ndiaye, Noémie. "Rewriting the *Grand Siècle*: Blackface in Early Modern France and the Historiography of Race." *Literature Compass* 18, no. 10 (2021). https://doi.org/10.1111/lic3.12603.

A compelling argument for how ignoring the presence of blackface performance in seventeenth-century France (preceding the court ballets of Lully) has led to inaccurate historiographies on race in multiple disciplines. Ndiaye also argues that scholars should use interdisciplinary methods and sources to understand a topic as complex as race. This article is useful for instructors who wish to transfer similar arguments to music history. Although Ndiaye writes about court ballet in this instance, she is a literary historian; thus, this article is also a good model for how researchers and students can cross disciplinary boundaries.

Florence Price

Brown, Rae Linda, and Guthrie P. Ramsey. *The Heart of a Woman: The Life and Music of Florence B. Price*. Music in American Life. Urbana, IL: University of Illinois Press, 2020.

This is a detailed study of composer Florence Price, including her earliest years, her family background, her education, her career, and analysis of major works. I recommend that instructors assign several chapters pertaining to Price's upbringing in Little Rock, AK, and her early career. Chapter 6 ("Clark University and Marriage," pp. 74–85), discusses early teaching and her pedagogical piano pieces including *Dances in the Canebrakes*, set against the continued racial violence in Little Rock, especially death threats against Price's family. Chapter 14 ("Performing Again," pp. 176–84), returns to similar themes at the height of Price's career, with discussion of her charitable fundraising work through performance, and discussion and analysis of her lesser known but brilliant organ compositions; this chapter also narrates the struggles that Black communities in the South faced while trying to access high-quality public education. Together, these two chapters can help students understand how much Price's career (and those of other prominent and everyday contemporaries) was impacted by racism.

Chapters 10–12 are also valuable as reading assignments; I recommend using these as the basis for a longer unit, while branching out into related topics. Chapter 10 ("Spirituals to Symphonies: A Century of Progress," pp. 117–25) includes background on African-American composers working in classical music, with quotations from primary source reviews of Price's *Symphony in E Minor*. Chapter 11 ("The Symphony in E Minor," pp. 126–54) includes a brief history of Black composers in classical music before Florence Price and discusses the use of American-Indian and "Negro" melodies as a form of "nationalism" in music. (See Horowitz 2001, Nicholls 2008, Ndiaye 2021 in Chapter 4 for more sources on the Indianist phase in American music.) This chapter concludes with an analysis of Price's use of the juba as a dance form in large- and small-scale works, including in "Silk Hat and Walking Cane" from *Dances in the Canebrakes*. Chapter 12 ("O Sing a New Song," pp. 155–64) analyzes *Dances in the Canebrakes* in more detail.

Holloway, Joseph E., ed. *Africanisms in American Culture*. Blacks in the Diaspora. Bloomington: Indiana University Press, 2005.

This volume includes several essays worth assigning for class, or using as lecture builders. Several essays address the origins of African-American dance, including the juba, which is relevant for studying Price's *Dances in the Canebrakes*.

Schenbeck, Lawrence. "Music, Gender, and 'Uplift' In the 'Chicago Defender,' 1927–1937." *The Musical Quarterly* 81, no. 3 (1997): 344–70.

This article contains quotations from primary sources with reviews of Price's compositions in Chicago; to facilitate students' use of primary sources, assign this article together with Chapter 10 ("Spirituals to Symphonies") of Brown's *The Heart of a Woman*, described above. (See In-Class Listening Exercise, Case Study 7.)

Von Glahn, Denise. *Music and the Skillful Listener: American Women Compose the Natural World*. Bloomington, IN: Indiana University Press, 2013.

A wonderful interpretation that turns stereotypical associations with women and nature into a much more profitable study that also addresses listening practices. Several chapters discuss women composers in the symphonic idiom, that can serve as corollaries to Florence Price in a longer module (Box 3.10.)

Muddy Waters

Baldwin, Clive. *Anxious Men: Masculinity in American Fiction of the Mid-Twentieth Century*. Edinburgh: Edinburgh University Press, 2020.

Chapter 5 ("African American Identity and Masculinity," pp. 196–234) places Muddy Waters' "Mannish Boy" into a literary tradition of Black anxieties about masculinity. Although the chapter is not music focused, the material could be useful as a reading or discussion prompt (combined with some short excerpts from the additional literature discussed) in advanced classes.

Gioia, Ted. *Delta Blues: The Life and Times of the Mississippi Masters Who Revolutionized American Music*. New York: W. W. Norton, 2009.

Written in an accessible, engaging style, this book features Muddy Waters in several chapters, especially pp. 200–205, 220–30; I recommend this work as a reading assignment at all levels.

Smith, Ayana. "Blues, Criticism, and the Signifying Trickster." *Popular Music* 24, no. 2, Literature and Music (2005): 179–91.

Although this article does not discuss Muddy Waters, it provides context for how blues musicians developed authorial voice. For survey classes, this article would offer background on the themes and musical features of blues repertory; for advanced classes, have students use the "signifying trickster" framework to develop their own interpretations.

4 Caricature and Character, Appropriation and Authenticity

Chapter 4 examines the limits, and problems, associated with appropriating others' cultures by juxtaposing works by Amy Marcy Cheney Beach (1867–1944) and Brent Michael Davids (b. 1959; Stockbridge-Munsee Mohican) and engaging with music from two perspectives: borrowed compositional materials versus authentic intercultural voice. Here we continue the perspective building begun in Chapter 3, but now focusing less on the medium of representation (image, text, music, opera, etc.) and more on the mechanisms of cultural appropriation, while modelling curricular intervention strategies. The musical examples chosen offer opportunities to consider land, landscape, and place with respect to identity. Such connections challenge researchers, instructors, and students alike to think more contextually about musical and political relationships in the early twentieth-century U.S., such as: stereotypical representations, early academic ethnological studies, and government policies on land ownership. Making these historical associations explicit to the study of music encourages all of us to contend with challenging topics.

This chapter raises some thorny questions, including: How do we discuss the use of Native American melodies by non-Indigenous composers? Should we respond differently when underrepresented minorities (such as women composers) appropriate others' musical identities? How should we consider early ethnological studies of American Indian musics—work often done by women who were sometimes lacking institutional or academic support, but work also embodying inherited colonial attitudes? Instructors could expand on the case studies offered here by adding the following repertory-based discussions: When Amy Beach quotes American Indian melodies in *From Blackbird Hills* (1922), or in the *String Quartet, op. 89* (1929), which land or landscape is she referencing, what happened to that land, and how does it evoke "Americana"? How should we understand seemingly "abstract" art music (as in the *String Quartet*), when it is based on pre-existing materials that have specific meanings in another culture? (Box 4.1.)

DOI: 10.4324/9781003219385-4

> **Box 4.1: Syllabus Design; Authenticity and Appropriation**
>
> Create a module (or an entire course) on authenticity and appropriation, modeling Case Studies 6 (see Chapter 3), 9, and 10. Works such as Gershwin's *Porgy and Bess* (Chapter 2, Box 2.5) and Giacomo Puccini's *Madama Butterfly* (1904) represent prime examples of cultural borrowing; tailor additional examples to the goals of the course. For each instance of appropriation, include at least one instance of authentic (or intercultural) voice, focusing on a work from a similar genre by a marginalized composer. Contrast *Butterfly* with *Matsukaze* (2011), an opera by Toshio Hosokawa (b. 1955). Such pairings diversify the scope of a module, unit, or entire semester; while offering some favorite works from the music history canon, the theme now centers ethical considerations.

The aim is not to frame composers of the past from a position of hostility, since their contemporary ideas about using cultural materials were not the same as ours today. Rather, the aim is to study the cultural aesthetics and the belief systems that motivated it; how were belief systems influenced by ideologies about race, ethnicity, religion, and politics in that period?

To intervene in this system of musical cultural appropriation, making more visible what has been a shadow history in many music history classrooms, this chapter also discusses *By Our Nature* (2014), a work by well-known Indigenous composer Brent Michael Davids (Case Study 10). The goal is to bring forward the shadow histories of the various peoples whose cultures are currently represented in Western art music mainly through appropriative borrowings within the traditional canon. By revealing shadow histories, we highlight a diverse range of creative musical practices while demonstrating how marginalized composers represent their own communities through compositional or performative authority.

Ultimately, this chapter challenges us to rethink "What is American musical nationalism?" How do we define "American landscapes" in musical form?

Case Study 9: Amy Beach, *String Quartet, op. 89* (1929)

There are many scholarly challenges regarding the use of Native American melodies in Western art music; despite recent calls to decolonize curricula, gaps and ethical problems remain. Some scholarly literature on Amy Beach advances perspectives and terminology that we would now consider unbalanced and outdated. Without significantly updated scholarship, the predominant voice that students encounter foregrounds colonializing, romanticizing, and orientalizing viewpoints. Even within newer scholarship, we lack information that reifies the diverse perspectives of Indigenous peoples.

A similar disparity exists in the broader scholarly literature on the Indianist movement, formed when a group of composers at the turn of the twentieth century quoted or emulated Native American musics to convey what they considered a uniquely nationalist American sound. Some of this scholarship recognizes that the Indianist movement was part of a broader cultural appropriation and ethnic stereotyping that also occurred in film, literature, and other creative outlets;[1] yet there is very little discussion of Native American histories, cultures, or musics within the same scholarship to contextualize the simultaneous impact on the lives of Indigenous peoples.

Treating the lives of Native American peoples separately from how Western culture represents those lives, engenders a scholarly literature entirely based on Western, colonial perspectives. Historiography therefore perpetuates Western representations, even as we critique them using methods such as postcolonialism. This separation results in fractures—the opposite of inclusivity. Narratives that should be linked are treated as discrete topics or events—or even as separate disciplines.[2] Since students may not take an anthropology, sociology, ethnomusicology, or American Indian studies class while they are enrolled in our music history classes, I believe it is ethically imperative to include a holistic history in our scholarship and teaching—one that centers Indigenous peoples as much as we are able.

Ignoring historical simultaneities allows an origin myth/shadow history structure to develop. As musicologists, we have been lulled into a sense of "safety;" we collectively forget to mention that wars against American Indians continued west of the Mississippi into the twentieth century, overlapping with the Indianist movement in American music. Local battles such as the Battle of Bear Valley, the Posey War, and the final episodes of the Apache Wars did not conclude until 1918, 1923, and 1924, respectively. Ongoing land disputes, settler colonialism, and governmental land redistribution projects reduced Indigenous peoples' land access and political autonomy by both *de facto* and *de jure* actions.

Of course, it is also a valid teaching choice to exclude works by Beach (or other composers) that borrow American Indian musical ideas. We do not have to teach the *String Quartet* when we could teach the *Gaelic Symphony* (1894) or "Hermit Thrush at Morn" (1921). These latter pieces also meet the educational goals often associated with Beach or early American music, namely musical-cultural borrowing or the musical representation of nature and landscape; we might find these easier to contextualize by avoiding political conflicts. However, teaching Antonín Dvořák's influence on American music already opens the door to this fraught topic; the Indianist movement represents a significant aspect of Dvořák's legacy. If we do not broach these topics from the full perspective offered here, we essentially continue to shroud this period of American music in shadows. If we are willing to explore intersecting issues between music, politics, race, representation, land, and landscape, we enrich our students.

Syllabus Design: Women and the American Symphony

Consider a module on women as symphony composers in the U.S., centering works by Amy Beach, Florence Price (Chapter 3, Box 3.10), and Radie Britain (1899–1994). For additional repertory, see Van Glahn 2013, *Music and the Skillful Listener.*

Lecture Idea, Day 1: Amy Beach and Trends in American Music

Begin with background on the composer. Her social circumstances—a married woman from a privileged background, who began her musical education very young, performing as a child prodigy—can lead to discussions about class and gender expectations in late nineteenth and early twentieth-century music-making cultures. Despite her early promise, as an adult she was advised against formal composition study by her husband and trusted mentors. Upon marriage, Beach was prevented from continuing her performance career, other than for charitable purposes; she only resumed concert appearances after her husband's death, traveling to Europe for the first time later in life. Although our modern viewpoints lead us to interpret these biographical details from a perspective of restriction, Beach surpassed these seeming obstacles by developing her own voice—a construct that was much valued in her day, which male creatives also espoused. Her social class afforded her freedom to study. Beach's daily self-guided education in theory, composition, and nineteenth-century symphonic style led her on a successful career path. She became one of the earliest women composers in the U.S. to have symphonic works premiered by a major orchestra.

Beach belonged to the "Second New England School", a group including figures such as George Whitefield Chadwick (1854–1931), Edward MacDowell (1861–1908), and Horatio Parker (1863–1919), all based in or near Boston, Massachusetts. At this time, American composers debated about how to create a unique, identifiable, nationalistic sound. There were several approaches established to meet this goal: 1) use musical materials that represent ethnic groups present in the U.S. (influenced by Dvořák); 2) continue the late-Romantic European symphonic tradition, infused with new modernistic ideas, techniques, and harmonies; and 3) create musical representations of the natural environment. These strategies could exist separately or together in a composition, or across a composer's career.

A highly innovative composer, Beach accomplished all three. Although this case study focuses on Beach's use of American Indian melodies, her *Gaelic Symphony* also demonstrates how she used the

European symphonic tradition (particularly Dvořák's *New World Symphony*, 1893) as a model for quotations or emulations of ethnic folksong. Beach represented nature in her piano pieces "Hermit Thrush at Morn" and "Hermit Thrush at Eve" (1921), both associated with her residency at the MacDowell Colony. Beach's exacting ear enabled her to notate precise transcriptions from the natural environment, then place them into modern tonal contexts. Greater scholarly emphasis has been accorded to the exact capturing of birdsong by the later composer Olivier Messiaen (1908–1992); in the classroom, highlighting Beach's accomplishments in this area intervenes in a gendered historiographical imbalance. Beach's modernist harmonic frameworks are evident in the *String Quartet*; overall, Beach's varied compositional strategies have affinities with American literary movements, such as Transcendentalism (Ralph Waldo Emerson, 1803–1882; Henry David Thoreau, 1817–1862) and Realism (Walt Whitman, 1819–1892).

In-Class Activity

Conclude lecture with multiple listening examples. In small groups, analyze short literary passages drawn from Transcendentalism and Realism; discuss how they relate to Beach's compositional styles. Highlighting the varied layers of Beach's career—including relationships between music, landscape, culture, and literature—creates a musically rich classroom experience, while elevating a woman as a composer in a space often associated with men either collectively or individually in the music canon (i.e., symphonic music, modernism, birdsong transcriptions).

Lecture Idea, Day 2: The *String Quartet* and Borrowings from Native America

To create symmetry with the previous class (which began with lecture and concluded with group musical analysis), begin the second day with a discussion session and end with instructor summation of historical contexts.

In-Class Activity

In small groups, students engage with the source melodies quoted by Beach in her *String Quartet*.[3] Identify how Beach used this material formally, harmonically, and stylistically, using music theoretical terms.

During the second portion of the class, guide students to discuss the impacts of early publications documenting Native American melodies. Direct more advanced students to consider similarities between Indianist strategies in early twentieth-century American music and

80 *Caricature and Character, Appropriation and Authenticity*

> "cultural extractivism." Have students draw parallels between creating anthologies of ethnological music transcriptions and creating museum collections; both acts remove cultural materials from Indigenous peoples to be used as objects of study. (To incorporate a longer historical timeline on sonic and material collections, see Chapter 3, Case Study 6.)
>
> Conclude the class by summarizing the historically intersecting forces of music, ethnology, land disputes, and representation of identity.

Since Beach's *String Quartet* was based on materials collected by the early ethnographer Franz Boas (1858–1942), I recommend creating gender balance by concluding the class lecture with Alice Cunningham Fletcher (1838–1923), a prominent female ethnologist, whose book *A Study of Omaha Indian Music* influenced Beach's piano piece *From Blackbird Hills*. Ethnologists and early anthropologists—who were backed by powerful cultural, financial, and political institutions—often collected additional material items and oral narratives for other researchers while they were completing their own fieldwork. Thus, one person could have a significant influence on an entire body of knowledge, even when the resulting publications were written by different authors. This was indeed the case with Alice Cunningham Fletcher, whose work brought her to multiple tribal lands, and who shared collected materials with other researchers while also working for the U.S. government.

Although many female ethnologists worked for little or no compensation, Fletcher was employed by the Peabody Museum at Harvard University and received considerable fellowship funding for her fieldwork. She also served as a government agent in the Land Allotment of the Nez Perce Reservation in north-central Idaho, which resulted from the Dawes Severalty Act of 1887. Although some members of the Nez Perce Tribe participated in the land allotment process, many members were vigorously opposed to it. Those who participated may not have realized the ultimate effects, since the outcomes of government policies were often not made clear upfront. Students should understand the resulting effects on Native American lands and peoples; discuss the additional implications for scholarly objectivity when research and politics overlap. Students should also understand that although women were frequently discriminated against as composers and academics (and in other fields) during this era, they could also be agents of discrimination against those who had less institutional power.

The land allotment process granted individuals plots of land up to 160 acres, but ultimately decimated the communal land uses traditionally held by the Nez Perce Tribe. Simultaneously, the redistribution enabled the U.S. Government to remove unallotted plots away from the Tribal Reservation, thus diminishing the overall Nez Perce access to landscapes and altering land use; by "checkerboarding" the land, this legislation resulted in families being separated and ultimately being forced to give up their land.[4] This outcome was especially damaging since tribal members were often contending with settlers simultaneously encroaching on the area. Knowledge of such fraught political situations provides students with greater awareness of the jarring contrasts inherent to early anthropological projects, and their impact on music history. Instructors can also present this scenario as a precursor to discussions about ethical research and curatorial processes, by assigning materials on the repatriation of museum objects.[5] How would students design similar collaborative mechanisms for research and performance fields? (See Box 4.2.)

Box 4.2: Discussion Topic—Curatorial Mindsets

What can musicians learn from the curatorial relationships between museums and Indigenous communities? Have students do background research (or assign a reading) on recent curatorial collaborations and their resulting exhibitions.

Instructors can bring knowledge of specific projects to the discussion. NAGPRA (Native American Graves Protection and Repatriation Act, 1990) is a federal law requiring the return of Native American cultural products to their tribal origins. Instructors may want to look for recent examples of university and museum collections that are collaborating with Native American communities to respectfully return objects in their collections; discuss the inherent problems with collections that hold personal objects such as voice recordings and photographs—which rightfully belong to heirs, who often cannot access them.

Adrienne Fried Block's work on Beach is a good entry point to these ideas.[6] Block discusses the representation of American Indian musics and cultures at the Chicago World's Columbian Exposition in 1893 in terms of a hierarchical, ethnic, and racial "landscape" reflecting Darwinian theories. Although Block does not use the term "scientific racism" in her article, students should learn this term, and recognize its operation in the primary source materials cited by Block. Fletcher had concluded her ethnological research and land allotment work on the Nez Perce Tribal Reservation earlier in the same year as the World's Columbian Exposition, where she then travelled to give several lectures on Indigenous American musics. Beach was also present at the Exposition; she likely would have seen the ethnological exhibits, perhaps even attended Fletcher's lectures while several of her works were performed at the fairgrounds. Understanding Fletcher's role in multiple spheres—musical, ethnological, governmental, and collectivist—provides students a more accurate context both for this historical moment, and for Beach's use of Native American melodies. (Box 4.3.)

> **Box 4.3: Reading Assignment and Discussion Prompts—Race and Music at the World's Fairs and Expositions**
>
> For an advanced topics class or graduate seminar, assign Block's article "Amy Beach's Music;" (Block 1990) alongside my "Like the Light of Liberty" article (André et al. 2020). Discuss how landscapes—whether outdoors, designed, constructed, institutional, or *de facto*—represent societal notions of race, class, ethnicity, gender, religion, or other identity groups. How did these dynamics impact musical performance at both the Chicago World's Columbian Exposition in 1893 and the Tennessee Centennial Exposition in 1897? How do similar dynamics surround us in our current landscapes and musical institutions?
>
> How do modern rituals, ceremonies, holidays, public gatherings, and musical performances, etc. help to define American nationalism(s) today? How should musicians develop ethical practices regarding studying, performing, and teaching musical materials by minoritized groups? What do we lose when trying to notate Indigenous musics using traditional Western theoretical tools? Instructors should help students understand that Native American peoples enjoy different relationships to song cultures compared to Western notions; for example, what are the inherent ethical problems when we attempt to create permanence (through recording or transcription) for songs that are considered living? (For more about song and listening practices, see Dylan Robinson, *Hungry Listening*.) How do Block's and Smith's articles engage with themes of authenticity and appropriation? Instructors may also wish to discuss the continuation of the "noble savage" tropes that were prevalent in the eighteenth century (Chapter 3, Case Study 6) into more recent eras.

Using a "layered pathway" approach, students could develop research-related projects on these themes; ask students to locate ethical, collaborative exhibits or digital archives that hold materials on Native American musics, and describe the collaborative process while providing more background on one or two objects.[7] (Box 4.4.) Or, have students work with the frameworks of "mapping" and "landscape" as demonstrated in several of the readings in the bibliography for this chapter. (Box 4.3.)

> **Box 4.4: Developing Research and Analysis Skills; Ethnology and Primary Sources**
>
> Have advanced students study the quoted Indigenous melodies in Beach's *String Quartet*. What musical techniques did Beach use to surround and contextualize the borrowed melodies (if possible, go beyond the discussion offered in Block)? Assign at least one of the articles or book chapters on Native American musics from the bibliography. What does the audience lose from the meaning(s) and cultural context(s) of Indigenous musics in Beach's presentation of the score? How does Beach's approach differ from the techniques used (or recommendations offered) by Dvořák or Chadwick? How does Beach's style and use of a generic title (*String Quartet*) separate her piece from others with more explicit titles, or from works by other composers who participated in the Indianist movement?

Case Study 10: Brent Michael Davids, *By Our Nature* (2014)

Even if we choose not to teach Dvořák and Beach from the perspectives delineated in Case Study 9, we should nevertheless commit to including music by Indigenous American composers in our courses. I have chosen to highlight Brent Michael Davids' short film score *By Our Nature* (2015). Perhaps one of the best-known composers of Indigenous American heritage, Brent Michael Davids is also a tireless advocate for other Native American composers and musicians. Among other important roles, Brent Michael Davids has founded the Native American Composer Apprentice Project, the Composer Apprentice National Outreach Endeavor, and helped organize the First Nations Composer Initiative while serving as its first Artistic Director.

In his compositions, Brent Michael Davids blends traditional instruments and sonic materials within forms derived from Western art music, a process that has been called "intercultural" or "transcultural."[8] His technique—while musically quite different—is structurally organized like that of William Grant Still (Chapter 1, Case Study 2) and Florence Price (Chapter 3, Case Study 7). He invented instruments that provide specific tone qualities reminiscent of Native American musics; among these are two crystal quartz flutes, and several percussion instruments.

By Our Nature is intended to be "performed" or played in a concert hall. This work highlights the importance of human connection to nature, the environment, and climate health. *By Our Nature* uses filmography to inspire the audience, presenting a utopian—but also real—vision of the world that surrounds us. Given that it should be viewed in a concert hall, we might also consider how pastoral nostalgia informs the work. The beautiful visual presentation of open nature would contrast significantly with the audience's urban, constructed, confined listening and viewing environment, and most likely with their regular living spaces. Perhaps the audience would even reflect on how their daily lives—transportation, work, building structures, etc.—interact with, support, or delimit environmental preservation and experiencing the natural world.

The prevalence of the wood flute in the score highlights the importance of this instrument to several Indigenous American musics, while the lyrical vocal refrain towards the conclusion reminds us of the importance of orality, songs, stories, and narrative in maintaining Indigenous cultural traditions. Instructors who assign this work could develop discussion questions about nature, land, landscapes, and Indigenous perspectives in the late nineteenth, early twentieth, and twenty first centuries. How can we enter these conversations respectfully—while contemplating the impacts on our current environments? Broadly speaking, how has the topic of nature served as a stereotype for women and Indigenous composers—while providing specific inspiration for composers such as Beach and Brent Michael Davids?

Notes

1 See, for example, Michael V. Pisani, *Imagining Native America in Music* (New Haven, CT: Yale University Press, 2008), https://doi.org/10.12987/yale/9780300108934.001.0001.
2 For example, see Chapter 1 and Chapter 9 in David Nicholls, *The Cambridge History of American Music* (Cambridge: Cambridge University Press, 2008), https://doi.org/10.1017/CHOL9780521454292. While Chapter 1 presents a broad history of Native American musics, Chapter 9 discusses the Indianist movement without reference to the historical simultaneities for Indigenous musics, or how government policies and academic ethnology shaped Indigenous lives.
3 Adrienne Fried Block, "Amy Beach's Music on Native American Themes," *American Music* 8, no. 2 (1990): 141–66.
4 Many thanks to Breana H. McCullough, who informed me of the effects of checkerboarding.
5 Some important resources on this topic include Kimberly Christen, "Opening Archives: Respectful Repatriation," *The American Archivist* 74, no. 1 (2011): 185–210; Saul, Gwendolyn, and Ruth Jolie, "Inspiration from Museum Collections: An Exhibit as a Case Study in Building Relationships between Museums and Indigenous Artists," *American Indian Quarterly* 42, no. 2 (2018): 246–70.
6 Block, "Amy Beach's Music."
7 For some resources, see: Haley Gallagher and Iris Bennett, "Off the Shelf and into the Conversation: Indigenous Music and Shared Stewardship," *Smithsonian Center for Folklife & Cultural Heritage* (blog), October 2, 2020, https://folklife.si.edu/magazine/indigenous-music-shared-stewardship; John Vallier, "Community Collaboration in Ethnomusicology Archives: Ethical Considerations for Collections Management," *ARSC Journal* 52, no. 1 (2021): 117–24; and Ricardo L. Punzalan and Diana E. Marsh, "Reciprocity: Building a Discourse in Archives,"

The American Archivist 85, no. 1 (2022): 30–59, https://doi.org/10.17723/2327-9702-85.1.30.

8 Dale A. Olsen, "Globalization, Culturation, and Transculturation in American Music: From Cultural Pop to Transcultural Art," in *Reflections on American Music: The Twentieth Century and the New Millennium: A Collection of Essays Presented In Honor of the College Music Society*, CMS Monographs and Bibliographies in American Music 16 (Hillsdale, N.Y.: Pendragon Press, 2000).

Annotated Bibliography

Racial Landscapes

André, Naomi and Denise Von Glahn (Convenors), Gwynne Kuhner Brown, Marva Griffin Carter, Tammy L. Kernodle, Horace J. Maxile, Ayana Smith, Kristen M. Turner, and Josephine R. B. Wright. "Colloquy: Shadow Culture Narratives: Race, Gender, and American Music Historiography." *Journal of the American Musicological Society* 73, no. 3 (December 1, 2020): 711–84. https://doi.org/10.1525/jams.2020.73.3.711.

My contribution to this colloquy, "Like the Light of Liberty: Art, Music, and Politics at the 1897 Tennessee State Fair and the Long History of African American Music," (pp. 724–40) provides a counterpoint to Block's approach ("Amy Beach's Music") in analyzing the musical and cultural landscapes at a fairground, demonstrating the underlying racial attitudes that impacted musical creation. (Box 4.3.)

Junka-Aikio, Laura, and Catalina Cortes-Severino. "Cultural Studies of Extraction." *Cultural Studies* 31, no. 2–3 (May 4, 2017): 175–84. https://doi.org/10.1080/09502386.2017.1303397.

This overview article (the "Editorial" for a special double-issue journal volume) is a notable resource for instructors or advanced graduate students on the topic of cultural "extractivism." Other articles in the same volume might also be useful; although the topics tend to be more about land-based resources, some of the scholarship refers to digital resources, and cultural and political implications, providing methodological models for music research.

Amy Beach

Block, Adrienne Fried. "Amy Beach's Music on Native American Themes." *American Music* 8, no. 2 (1990): 141–66.

By contrast to the Horowitz article ("Reclaiming the Past"), Block contextualizes how Beach encountered American Indian musics, the primary sources she used, and the racial hierarchies represented at the Chicago World's Columbian Exposition in 1893, which Beach attended. Block presents background on Indigenous American thematic material in the *String Quartet*. I recommend assigning this article to students (or using it to build a lecture). (see Box 4.3.) This article overlaps in methodology with the "Racial Landscapes" category, above.

Horowitz, Joseph. "Reclaiming the Past: Musical Boston Reconsidered." *American Music* 19, no. 1 (2001): 18–38.

Provides context for understanding the Boston musical climate at the turn of the twentieth century; discusses several composers, conductors, and performers, including Amy Beach, George Whitefield Chadwick, Teresa Carreño, among others. A section on Dvořák's borrowings leads to discussion of the Indianist movement in American history. I do not recommend assigning this article to students, however, since it uses outdated language while romanticizing and orientalizing cultural appropriation without engaging in relevant perspective building; Horowitz characterizes women in ways that would be considered offensive today (for example, referring to Amy Beach as a "marital trophy.") It might be fruitful to assign this article in a graduate seminar, by creating a targeted exercise in recognizing layers of the "Mimesis to Mockery" framework in scholarship (see Chapter 3, esp. Figure 3.1).

Nicholls, David. *The Cambridge History of American Music*. Cambridge: Cambridge University Press, 2008. https://doi.org/10.1017/CHOL9780521454292.

Chapter 9 ("Art Music from 1860–1920," pp. 214–54) has a valuable section on American musical nationalism (pp. 249–53); Dvořák and the Chicago Exposition are considered leading influences in the folk-derived musical borrowing underpinning the Indianist movement, discussed together with Amy Beach. Assign as preparatory reading for students at the survey level who may not be ready for Block, Smith, or critical methodological engagement. Instructors can use more advanced readings to construct lecture materials instead of using them as course assignments.

Von Glahn, Denise. *Music and the Skillful Listener: American Women Compose the Natural World*. Bloomington, IN: Indiana University Press, 2013.

Chapter 2 ["Amy Marcy Cheney Beach (Mrs. H.H.A. Beach);" pp. 32–47] focuses on Beach's engagement with nature—especially the piano piece "Hermit Thrush at Morn;" appropriate for all educational levels, this chapter is especially suited for undergraduate survey classes, or a course on women composers. In a survey class, instead of separating identities across the syllabus, pair this repertory with William Grant Still's *Kaintuck* (Chapter 1, Case Study 2); shifting the focus to landscape in early twentieth-century American music would be a powerful intervention against tokenism.

Early Ethnologies and Land History

Please note: While I offer these early ethnological writings on Native American cultures and musics, I do not recommend them for instructional use (except perhaps Francis La Flesche (1857–1932), who wrote about his own culture from his own perspective). However, I think it is important to understand that these exist; we might profitably think of these as akin to a blackface minstrelsy version of scholarship (I recognize this analogy is not exact, but I wish to provoke discussions of authenticity and inauthenticity in representation and appropriation of culture)—these sources portray Native American cultures from patronizing and stereotypical perspectives, without the collaboration or reciprocity expected under today's ethical guidelines. It might be possible, under very carefully contextualized circumstances, for an advanced graduate student to reference these works using the "Mimesis to Mockery" framework, especially when using authentic Native American primary sources and scholarship as a counterbalance. Even then, authors must be very careful about methodology and tone.

Boas, Franz. "The Central Eskimo." In *Sixth Annual Report of the Bureau of Ethnology to the Secretary of the Smithsonian Institution, 1884–1885*, 399–669. Washington, DC: Government Printing Office, 1888. https://repository.si.edu/handle/10088/91644.

Several of the musical melodies collected by Franz Boas during his ethnological study of Alaskan Inuit peoples were quoted by Amy Beach in her *String Quartet*. The section on "Poetry and Music" in Boas' publication begins on p. 648.

Fletcher, Alice C., and Francis La Flesche. *A Study of Omaha Indian Music*. Cambridge, MA: Peabody Museum of American Archeology and Ethnology, 1893. https://library.si.edu/digital-library/book/studyofomahaindi00flet.

Modern editions of this work include helpful introductions and other scholarly tools; the link included here points to the Smithsonian Library's 1893 edition. Read more about the wax cylinder recordings that Fletcher made of Omaha Indian music, the transcription process, and how the harmonies were created here: https://www.loc.gov/static/collections/omaha-indian-music/articles-and-essays/omaha-indian-music-album-booklet/omaha-indian-music.html

La Flesche, Francis. *Ke-Ma-Ha: The Omaha Stories of Francis La Flesche*. Bison Books Imprint, 1998.

A first-person account of Omaha Indian culture interlaced with biographical narrative. The first professional Native American ethnologist, La Flesche (1857–1932) was a member of the Omaha Indian Tribe who also worked for the Smithsonian Institute and collaborated with Alice Cunningham Fletcher. For a shorter description of La Flesche's work, including his collaboration with Fletcher, see the Library of Congress: https://www.loc.gov/item/ihas.200196221/

Land Histories

Kilpatrick, Jacquelyn. *Celluloid Indians: Native Americans and Film*. Lincoln: University of Nebraska Press, 1999.

The first chapter ("Genesis of the Stereotypes," pp. 1–16) provides a succinct analysis of the early historical factors that led to persistent stereotypes about Native Americans, including letters and documents by colonists, fictional narratives, Wild West shows, and the impacts of nationalism and the Land Removal Act (1830). This reading is essential for understanding how origin myth/shadow history dynamics develop, and how they become imprinted in cultural narratives. I recommend this chapter for all students and instructors; this chapter could be paired with Pisani, Chapter 5. For advanced classes, students could compare these negative stereotypes to portrayals of Native Americans in musical works, such as Rameau's "*Les Sauvages*" (Chapter 3, Case Study 6).

In the remainder of the book, author Jacquelyn Kilpatrick (Choctaw, Cherokee, Irish) discusses stereotypical depictions in chronology, in addition to authentic portrayals developed by Native American filmmakers. Selected readings from this book would help students (especially in advanced coursework) utilize the "Mimesis to Mockery" framework emphasized in this chapter; these readings would work well alongside discussions of appropriation versus "cultural" and "transcultural" voices as in Olsen (below).

Pisani, Michael V. *Imagining Native America in Music*. New Haven, CT: Yale University Press, 2008. https://doi.org/10.12987/yale/9780300108934.001.0001.

Chapter 5, "Ethnographic Encounters," traces early researchers' interactions with various Native American Tribes, influencing the Indianist movement. The central section of this chapter focuses on how academic ethnology developed (pp. 164–81) and how American Indians were portrayed at State and World's Fairs. This book incorporates a wide chronological span, from the seventeenth century to the present, discussing stereotypical ways of imagining Indigenous Americans in music-related genres from opera to film. I do not recommend using this book beyond Chapter 5 for classroom instruction; it focuses too much on negative portrayals without offering any kind of balance from Native American perspectives. While it is important to document these appropriative uses of Native American culture, there needs to be more contextualization to avoid the reification of falsified versions of identity.

Ruppel, Kristin T. *Unearthing Indian Land: Living with the Legacies of Allotment*. Tucson: University of Arizona Press, 2008.

This offers a thorough history and legal analysis of the Land Allotment policies of the U.S. government, with testimonies from those who continue to be impacted. This book provides important background for understanding the complex mechanisms of Native American land disenfranchisement that Alice Cunningham Fletcher (and others) helped to propagate. Although instructors may want to assign excerpts to advanced graduate students, principally this book will serve as knowledge background or lecture building; upon reading this book, instructors will be able to offer more nuanced feedback or structure to class discussions surrounding the political aspects of works like Amy Beach's *String Quartet* (and others based on Native American musics).

Brent Michael Davids

Garrett, Charles Hiroshi, Carol J. Oja, and Michigan Publishing (University of Michigan), eds. *Sounding Together: Collaborative Perspectives on U.S. Music in the 21st Century*. Ann Arbor, MI: University of Michigan Press, 2021. https://doi.org/10.3998/mpub.11374592.

Chapter 1, "Music in Unexpected Places: Hearing New Histories of Early American Music," (pp. 21–50) by Sarah Eyerly and Rachel Wheeler, examines early Indigenous American-hymnody, including a modern harmonization of a Lutheran chorale tune composed by Brent Michael Davids. This chapter contextualizes the breadth of Brent Michael Davids' career and can help instructors diversify classes on early music topics (see Chapter 1).

Knight, David B. *Landscapes in Music: Space, Place, and Time in the World's Great Music. Why of Where*. Lanham, MD: Rowman & Littlefield Publishers, 2006.

A brief section of Chapter 5 ("Imagined and Mythic Landscapes," pp. 148–81) discusses Brent Michael Davids' work *Welcome to PauWau: A Gathering of Nations* (2000).

Caricature and Character, Appropriation and Authenticity

Include this as a reading and listening assignment for a module on music and place, or on landscapes by composers from diverse backgrounds. Doing so encourages students to think about "Americana" themed works from the perspectives of marginalized peoples instead of only from the majority perspective. Discussions could address questions such as: who owns the land? What does it mean to be "American"? How do we define "nationalism"?

Olsen, Dale A. "Globalization, Culturation, and Transculturation in American Music: From Cultural Pop to Transcultural Art." In *Reflections on American Music: The Twentieth Century and the New Millennium: A Collection of Essays Presented In Honor of the College Music Society*. CMS Monographs and Bibliographies in American Music 16. Hillsdale, NY: Pendragon Press, 2000.

This chapter defines the author's views on shifts in American music beyond the term "globalization." One brief section on Brent Michael Davids is the longest piece of scholarly writing I could find on this celebrated contemporary composer (pp. 270, 282–284). Olsen considers Brent Michael Davids a "cultural" composer, since he uses influences from his own Native American (Stockbridge Mohecan) identity, and a "transcultural" composer because he blends this heritage with instruments, forms, and harmonies from the Western art music tradition. It should be noted that Olsen only uses the term "cultural" to describe heritage influences used by members of non-dominant or non-majority population groups in the U.S.

While Florence Price and William Grant Still would also satisfy Olsen's definition of "cultural"/"transcultural" (see Chapter 1, Case Study 2, and Chapter 3, Case Study 7), Amy Beach would not. Amy Beach borrowed from a European/immigrant heritage for the *Gaelic Symphony*, and quoted from a marginalized heritage for the *String Quartet*. This is an important distinction that can help students understand the differences between "borrowing" and "appropriation" on the one hand (George Gershwin, Amy Beach), and "transculturation" (William Grant Still, Florence Price, Brent Michael Davids) on the other hand.

Indigenous American Musics

Browner, Tara, ed. *Music of the First Nations: Tradition and Innovation in Native North America*. Music in American Life. Urbana: University of Illinois Press, 2009.

This is a broad collection of essays on Native American musics from diverse regional and tribal backgrounds and genres, using a variety of methodologies, such as linguistic, ethnographic, historical, narrative, and musical analysis. Since the whole collection could be used as an undergraduate survey class textbook, any of the individual chapters would be useful as background reading for several class days on Indigenous American musics. Includes many tables, transcriptions, and illustrations.

Keillor, Elaine, Tim Archambault, and John M. H. Kelly. *Encyclopedia of Native American Music of North America*. Santa Barbara, CA: Greenwood, 2013. https://publisher.abc-clio.com/9780313055065/5.

This book is a collaboration between scholars and musicians who are Native American (Tim Archambault, Kichesipirini Algonquin First Nation; John M. H. Kelly, Skidegate Haida, Eagle Clan of the Haida Nation of British Columbia) and non-Native (Elaine

Keillor); use as a textbook or as a reference source to expand lectures. The entries are organized by region, genre, or musical style; by song type or theme; by instrument; and by artist name. Assign the introduction ("Historical Overview of Native Americans and their Music," pp. xi–xlx) for a survey class (or for any students new to this subject). The first half of the essay discusses the history of First Peoples, while the second half reviews the early scholarship on Native American musics (beginning on p. xxv), including Franz Boas ("Ethnomusicology and Native American Music," (p. xxx.); a separate section discusses early female ethnologists, including Alice Cunningham Fletcher (beginning on p. xxxiii). This reading pairs well with Case Study 9 and Box 4.4. One of the historiographical challenges evident in this essay is that the second half (discussions of historical music making traditions) derives entirely from accounts of European settlers. Instructors should discuss how relational positionality and cultural extractivism impact history writing; how should we re-evaluate early ethnographies from these perspectives?

A short biographical essay on Brent Michael Davids, with some additional bibliographical references, begins on p. 273. Assign the entry on "Film Music" (p. 294) alongside *By Our Nature*. The sections on "Aerophones (Flutes and Whistles)," (pp. 231–34) and on "Flute Players and Performances" (pp. 296–98) contextualize the instrumentation choices in Brent Michael Davids' *By Our Nature*. Assign "Pow Wow Songs of Northern Style" (pp. 372–77) and "Pow Wow Songs of Southern Style" (pp. 378–82) with Brent Michael Davids' *Welcome to PauWau: A Gathering of Nations* (see above). Discuss the cultural stereotypes that have arisen about this sacred ritual.

Perea, Jessica Bissett. *Sound Relations: Native Ways of Doing Music History in Alaska*. 1st ed. Oxford University Press, 2021. https://doi.org/10.1093/oso/9780190869137.001.0001.

Jessica Bissett Perea (Dena'ina) provides exactly the intervention needed to Michael Pisani's book *Imaging Native America in Music*. The author considers issues of recorded archives and performances, contrasting colonial with Indigenous-centered ways of representing and listening to Native American musics. Jessica Bissett Perea emphasizes the importance of music historical research and sound studies *with*, *by*, and *for* Native American or Indigenous peoples.

Perea, John-Carlos. *Intertribal Native American Music in the United States: Experiencing Music, Expressing Culture*. Global Music Series. New York: Oxford University Press, 2014.

The author, John-Carlos Perea (Mescalero Apache, Irish, German, Chicano), introduces the concept of "soundings" as community-oriented music making and listening. In this book, John-Carlos Perea discusses intercultural and intertribal aspects of the traditional powwow and other genres; chapters 2 and 3 would be especially helpful for contextualizing some of the musical references found in Brent Michael Davids' *Welcome to PauWau* (see readings from Knight and Keillor et al.). Chapters 4 and 5 focus on activism and unexpectedness in Native American popular music and jazz. Includes a CD of recorded music examples discussed in the book.

Robinson, Dylan. *Hungry Listening: Resonant Theory for Indigenous Sound Studies*. Indigenous Americas. Minneapolis: University of Minnesota Press, 2020.

The Introduction (pp. 1–36) provides an important framework on listening; Dylan Robinson (xwélméxw (Stó:lō)) defines how we listen from our ingrained, learned cultural backgrounds as the "positionalities of the listening encounter." Dylan Robinson discusses music from the perspective of "resource extraction" or "extractivism," a term that is also applicable to the materials found in Case Studies 6 (Chapter 3) and 9 (Chapter 4). Assign the introduction to graduate students, especially in a methodology-oriented class or seminar.

Chapter 3, "Contemporary Encounters between Indigenous and Early Music" (pp. 114–48), analyses different models of collaboration between baroque ensembles and First Nations composers and performers, from "integration" to "presentation and exchange," among others; Dylan Robinson discusses the pitfalls and accomplishments of each model. For lecture content or a reading assignment, this chapter provides thought-provoking listening and discussion opportunities, or can serve as the basis for designing an imaginary collaborative performance as a research project. (See also: Chapter 3, Case Study 6.)

Chapter 4, "Ethnographic Redress, Compositional Responsibility," (pp. 149–200) responds to the historical ethnographic transcription and recording of Indigenous musics as illustrated by Case Study 9. I recommend continuing discussions on "extractivism" over several class days. If instructors followed Case Study 6 (Chapter 3) or Case Study 9, they will now have had three separate occasions to discuss this topic in different contexts, creating a layered pathway pedagogical technique (Chapter 1).

Wright-McLeod, Brian. *The Encyclopedia of Native Music: More than a Century of Recordings from Wax Cylinder to the Internet.* Tucson: University of Arizona Press, 2005.

Brian Wright-McLeod's (Dakota/Anishnabe) book is a history of Native American musics from the perspective of recording practices. Includes a 3-CD set titled *The Soundtrack of a People.* Use for lecture-building content; pair with readings and discussions on early ethnology (Case Study 9), with Dylan Robinson's work on listening practices, Jessica Bissett Perea's chapters on performance, recording, and archives, and John-Carlos Perea's discussions of recorded examples (all listed above).

5 Signifying Meaning in African-American Music

Chapter 5 continues the discussion of landscape by juxtaposing art, music, and politics, with place. Jazz is now considered by many to be part of the Western art music canon, due to its widespread influence on various types of concert music; although jazz composers have written for orchestral, operatic, and church music idioms, the historical narratives surrounding the genre's development often still treat it as a separate category.

Rather than argue for one position or another (is jazz Western art music?), it is more fruitful to discuss jazz (and African-American musics more generally) from the perspective of Black intellectual, cultural, and theoretical paradigms. Pedagogical frameworks grounded in intellectual histories ensure methodological equity with other genres; for example, when we teach madrigals, we are likely to teach Renaissance rhetorical, text-setting principles to reveal the music's expressive shape. When we teach early opera, we are likely to teach how members of the Florentine Camerata mimicked ancient Greek music theory and theatrical declamation, and how Claudio Monteverdi developed the *seconda prattica* using new dissonances, eschewing traditional voice leading practices. When we teach Anton Webern, we are likely to explain Arnold Schoenberg's twelve-tone system. We ask students to analyze music using these aesthetic or theoretical knowledges.

What is the systemic discourse for analyzing African-American musics? There is no one comprehensive system that explains the corpus of African-American musics—yet. I have developed several frameworks for this purpose; combined with analytical pathways (blues chords, jazz chords, and form), these bring depth of understanding to individual works.

The primary framework in this chapter builds on my colloquy contribution titled "Like the Light of Liberty," published in the *Journal of the American Musicological Society*, which advocates for a "long history" approach to Black music (which I call the "long century").[1] The "long century" collapses generic divides between vernacular, popular, and concert styles, and emphasizes African-American epistemological and storytelling practices (double consciousness, signifying, etc.), while situating Black music into discursive narratives. The "long century" approach juxtaposes primary sources describing the complex landscape in which Black music exists, comparing authorial

DOI: 10.4324/9781003219385-5

voices both internal and external to African-American culture. Whether in scholarly or pedagogical contexts, this framework connects recurring discourses, thus identifying where our modern rhetorics repeat past logics that we thought we had left behind.

The "long century" of African-American music recognizes that Black music in the U.S. has its own history. Comprehending folk idioms, folk practices, oral narrative traditions, and material culture dating to the earliest recorded examples, elucidates the functionality of later Black musics of any genre. For Edward Kennedy "Duke" Ellington (1899–1974), or for jazz in general, the "long century" approach brings improvisation from other cultural practices and narrative formats into the analytical frame: quilting, playing the dozens, call-and-response, and verbal rhetorics, all combine with layered instrumentation practices, the twelve-bar blues, and the thirty-two-bar popular song form.

The "long century" approach includes within it several theoretical paradigms, developed by me, and by others. The "signifying trickster" theory recognizes that African-American authorship centers hidden meanings, linguistic masking, ironic rhetorical strategies, or quotations placed into new contexts to create new, satirizing or oppositional, outcomes.[2] "Double consciousness" posits that African-Americans developed dual frameworks for conceiving or representing the self.[3] The "Like the Light of Liberty" paradigm (Smith 2005) places the music of Black Americans into conceptual landscapes, mapping related events or creative outputs, to elucidate how Black authorial and creative voices used resistance to articulate their own agency. (Box 5.1.)

Box 5.1: Analysis and Discussion—Undoing Minstrelsy

Advanced students can begin formulating their own analytical outcomes using the "Like the Light of Liberty" framework, by placing African-American music, music theater, and film into the metaphorical "landscape" of minstrelsy. Students will need to engage the basic stereotypes and formats of blackface minstrelsy first; this is a sensitive topic and instructors should only allow open discussion of this material in classes where they believe the students can do so seriously and respectfully. In the early twentieth century, many African-American artists had to reference minstrelsy in some way, whether appealing to its popularity among audiences, or standing up against it. Many artists did so in ways that subverted the genre's stereotypes while increasing Black authorial agency.

Have students study Will Marion Cook's (1869–1944) *Clorindy, or The First Cakewalk* (1898; text by Paul Laurence Dunbar)—the first Broadway show with an all-Black cast—or analyze the characters played by George Walker, Adah Overton Walker, and Bert Williams in *In Dahomey* (1902), also by Will Marion Cook, with lyrics by Paul Laurence Dunbar and book by Jesse A. Shipp. Both works include a significant amount of satire and "signify" on the minstrelsy tradition. Use photos and film clips of Bert Williams to trace the origins of Black comedy; analyze the differences between "character" and "caricature" (Chapter 4). Explore Ellington's reversals of minstrelsy in his short film *Black and Tan* (1929), pairing this exercise with Case Study 7 on Florence Price(Chapter 3). How did these artists use reversals, masking, and trickster narratives to bring out their own authorial voices? By returning to the subject of race and representation several times during the semester, instructors create a "layered pathway" (Chapter 1).

An example of the "Like the Light of Liberty" framework that encompasses both research and instructional methods would be a project or classroom module focusing on Ellington's works about Harlem ("Harlem River Quiver," 1927; "Harlem Speaks," 1933/1935; "Echoes of Harlem," 1936; *Harlem Airshaft*, 1940; *Harlem*, 1950). Each would be historicized according to primary source materials, creative works, newspapers, advertisements, political events, art exhibits, photographs, etc. revolving around, or about Harlem. The second version of "Harlem Speaks" (1935) could be juxtaposed against the Harlem race riot of the same year, literature about Harlem by Black authors who lived through this period (see Child 2019, Fisher 1927), the 1936 Mayor's Commission Report about the neighborhood's structural needs that was ordered by Mayor Fiorello LaGuardia (1882–1947) but remains unpublished, or later sources that represent the outcomes in Harlem after this period, such as Langston Hughes' *Montage of a Dream Deferred* (1951). This project could be adapted in length and difficulty according to the level of the course.

This list represents just a short starting point. What do these sources "say" or "speak" about Harlem, individually or collectively? What do these works tell us about freedom of voice, movement, and creativity, about impediments to freedom caused by landscape or environment? What is the "map" that defines, activates, or juxtaposes events that influence authorial voice? An innovative pedagogical approach to a topic such as this, especially for advanced undergraduate or graduate students, would be to devote an extended unit in which each student, working in pairs or small groups, contributes a brief research component using only 1–2 primary sources—analyzing them according to one of the paradigms discussed here—that are then placed on a digital map, or organized into a digital network graph. (See Box 5.2.)

> **Box 5.2: Reading and Discussion Assignment—Composers' Voices**
>
> Assign selections from the *Duke Ellington Reader* and the series of articles on Ellington in *The New Yorker* in 1944 by Richard Boyer. Have students analyze the sources for how Ellington describes himself versus how he is described by others, to gain a sense of "doubleness" in the composer-performer's legacy. Have students identify five keywords or phrases from the reading and write a brief report (no more than 250–500 words) explaining why they chose those keywords, their significance, and how the author used them to convey something about Ellington, his career, or his musical style. Have students bring a copy of their work as a "ticket to enter," and to use in "think-pair-share" exercises at the beginning of the class period.

This paradigm invokes comparative analysis, but goes further, contrasting "double consciousness" among Black authors, with a corresponding "doubleness" among white authors about Black culture. Advocating for a neighborhood by ordering a systematic study, but then not implementing the expert solutions is a form of "doubleness," as in the LaGuardia instance. The resulting interpretation reveals a new shadow history. What can this exercise teach us about how origin myths propagate stereotypes? Where do we find similar rhetorics or representations in our modern landscapes?

Case Study 11: Duke Ellington, *Harlem Airshaft* (1940)

Duke Ellington composed over 2,000 pieces in his lifetime; he was known for his industrious work ethic, composing new songs at night, then slipping them under the doorframes of his band members for the next day's performance or recording session. He composed sixteen new lines of music each day. Beyond his works for jazz band, Ellington wrote for film and symphony orchestras. Arriving in New York City in 1923, Ellington became part of the vibrant musical arts community in Harlem, contributing to the intellectual movement now known as the Harlem Renaissance.

> **Syllabus Design**
>
> Design a unit on the Harlem Renaissance period (1920s–1930s), engaging art, literature, and music. Include composers such as Florence Price (Chapter 3, Case Study 7), William Grant Still (Chapter 1, Case Study

2), Duke Ellington, and Muddy Waters (Chapter 3, Case Study 8), creating symmetry between two composers who worked primarily in art music, and two who worked primarily in popular musics.

Lecture Idea, Day 1

Ensure that your students understand that although the Harlem Renaissance is named after the famous neighborhood in New York City, it was a nationwide phenomenon occurring in large urban centers such as Chicago and Los Angeles, as well as in smaller metropolitan areas.

The Harlem Renaissance was not motivated by a single idea or course of action, but an innovative period of diverse ideologies merging to chart a new path. These new paths aimed to improve the lives of African Americans as they forged new possibilities in urban environments after the failures of the Reconstruction, followed by the heavy Jim Crow laws. Moreover, this was not a movement solely devoted to the arts, but also sought improved education, economic recovery, and better sociological outcomes. Learning (in brief) about the major intellectuals associated with this movement (Booker T. Washington, 1856–1915; Alain Locke, 1868–1954; W.E.B. DuBois, 1868–1963; Zora Neale Hurston, 1891–1960) will enforce the diversity of approaches developed to reach these goals.

Discuss such key ideas as articulated by "The Atlanta Compromise," (Washington, 1895; see Smith, 2020), "double consciousness" (DuBois), and "The New Negro" (Locke, and others), to contextualize the intellectual history supporting the Harlem Renaissance. Although Washington did not advocate for political action or greater civil rights, he did push for improved economic security through learning skilled trades. As the first president of the Tuskegee Institute in Alabama, Washington recognized the role of practical education in solving the great economic need among African Americans in the immediate post-slavery generations. Washington advocated for Black people to seek economic power through technological, industrial advancements, urging them to become central to a capitalist work force. Although many scholars today view this sentiment as outmoded (and patronizing) even for its time, the Great Migration was motivated by thousands upon thousands of African Americans doing just this—moving north (midwest and west) from rural areas in the South to urban areas, seeking new economic opportunities.

DuBois held opposite views; he advocated for racial equality, pushing for an elite liberal arts and science education, especially for the group he considered "The Talented Tenth." As a sociologist, he spoke out against the illogical, demeaning forces of race-based prejudice and discrimination, thus counteracting the strong forces of scientific racism. In his essay "Strivings of the Negro People," DuBois described the psychological impact of racism on Black people, using the expression "double consciousness." Black people, even as young as childhood, had to develop a second sense of identity, viewing, and presenting themselves according to the perspectives of white people—even though it was also damaging—in order to survive in the world. "The New Negro" was a term coined by Alain Locke as the title of an edited book in 1925, but many writers contributed to the meaning of this term; Black creatives developed characters that represented the "new" urban, sophisticated, middle to upper middle-class ideal. (There was *always* an elite, affluent Black class in the U.S. in both the North and the South—in the South, the timeframe was delayed until after the Civil War, although, due to Jim Crow laws, acquired wealth became tenuous there; in the North, elite families existed prior to the Civil War.)

The Harlem Renaissance movement involved a major push towards civil rights that did not culminate in political reality until the Civil Rights Act of 1964; however, a further repeal of the Jim Crow-era restrictions on voting did not pass until later, in 1965. Include the history of organizations and publications associated with the Harlem Renaissance; images or article excerpts from the National Association for the Advancement of Colored People (NAACP), *Crisis Magazine*, *Opportunity Magazine*, and the *Chicago Defender* would enrich the lecture.

Activity

Have students respond to two artworks revealing different manifestations of Harlem Renaissance aesthetics. Augusta Savage's (1892–1962) sculpture made for the New York World's Fair of 1939 titled *Lift Every Voice and Sing/The Harp* portrays a distinct characterization of African-American community compared to Palmer Hayden's (1890–1973) painting *The Subway* (c. 1930). Interestingly, Savage met Hayden in Paris; both belonged to a vibrant, constantly changing community of African-American artists, writers, and musicians there. Create a "think-pair-share" exercise; for each painting separately—or in larger groups each assigned to one painting, students first spend a few minutes writing down keywords or short phrases of what the painting says to them, then they share those reflections with a partner. How do these artists portray the relationships between the individual and community?

Next, students share with the whole class how the paintings' aesthetics connect with aspects of Harlem Renaissance ideologies: How did the artists use different techniques to realize similar goals? How did the artists envision African-American life? How did they critique reality through art? How do both artists exhibit "double consciousness," or "signify" on existing tropes? Based on these paintings, what are the ideal versus real characteristics—or situations—pertaining to the "New Negro"? For advanced classes, assign articles or excerpts by Alain Locke, W.E.B. DuBois, and other major thinkers or writers of the era to prepare for this activity.

Listening, Analysis, and Discussion, Day 2

How does Ellington musically portray life in a Harlem apartment building in *Harlem Airshaft*? How does the "airshaft" connect yet divide residents)? How does Ellington "signify" through music, or portray "double consciousness"? How does the piece reflect the "long century" of African-American music? What role(s) do form and instrumentation play in conveying these frameworks?

Compare this work to other American musical landscapes—and soundscapes—studied in your class. Compare *Harlem Airshaft* to (brief) examples from Ellington's *Harlem* (1950), articulating similarities and differences in musical techniques used by the composer. What are the defining criteria of "jazz" versus "symphonic" music (*Harlem* was commissioned by Arturo Toscanini, intended for performance by the New York Symphony)—location of performance? Form? Instrumentation? Concept? The educational or performance background of the musicians who play it?

Although this book concludes here, with Duke Ellington and the Harlem Renaissance, this is not at all the end of the story. It is my sincere wish that this book will continue to provoke new modes of scholarly and pedagogical activity showcasing works by diverse composers from all walks of life, beyond the case studies I have offered here—to create a truly inclusive history encompassing race, gender, religion, nationality, ethnicity, and disability. With the frameworks explained in this book, researchers and instructors will have an infinite variety to choose from, to add new perspectives, and new ways of thinking, analyzing music, and narrating its histories. Between creating "layered pathways," avoiding tokenism, and "shifting our thinking" about the goals of our curricula, we will never be done telling inclusive stories about music. It is also my sincere wish that the frameworks and strategies presented here will inspire new ways of doing scholarly writing, so that we all may join this project of creating research that supports inclusive music classrooms, studios, concert halls, public organizations, and communities.

Notes

1. Smith, "Like the Light of Liberty," contribution to Naomi André and Denise Von Glahn (Convenors) et al., "Colloquy: Shadow Culture Narratives: Race, Gender, and American Music Historiography," *Journal of the American Musicological Society* 73, no. 3 (December 1, 2020): 711–84, https://doi.org/10.1525/jams.2020.73.3.711. (See Chapter 4, bibliography, Box 4.1 for additional pedagogical strategies.)
2. Smith, "Blues, Criticism, and the Signifying Trickster," *Popular Music* 24, no. 2, Literature and Music (2005): 179–91. See also: Henry Louis Gates, *The Signifying Monkey: A Theory of African-American Literary Criticism*, 1. Oxford Univ. Press paperback, Oxford Paperbacks (New York, NY: Oxford Univ. Press, 1989) and Samuel A. Floyd, *The Power of Black Music: Interpreting Its History from Africa to the United States*, 1. iss. as paperback, Oxford Paperbacks (New York: Oxford Univ. Press, 1996).
3. W.E.B. DuBois, "Strivings of the Negro People," *The Atlantic Monthly* 80 (August 1897): 194–98.

Annotated Bibliography

Harlem and the Harlem Renaissance

Child, Ben. *The Whole Machinery: The Rural Modern in Cultures of the U.S. South, 1890–1946*. The New Southern Studies. Athens: The University of Georgia Press, 2019.

This book reverses the commonly-held paradigm that modernity originated in cities radiating outwards from there, arguing that through the Great Migration musical, literary, and artistic modernism derived from rural Southern practices, thence arriving in cities, such as New York, conveyed by African Americans. Chapter 5 ("Station to Station: New York City and the Returns of the Rural," pp. 159-200) includes a section about Harlem beginning on page 166. Duke Ellington's *Harlem Airshaft* is discussed as a counterpoint to Rudolph Fisher's (1897–1934) short story "The Promised Land" (1927), which features the airshaft almost as a character. Use this chapter to build a multi-media lecture (film, literature, music) on the Great Migration, with materials complementing Ellington's piece.

DuBois, W.E.B. "Strivings of the Negro People." *The Atlantic Monthly* 80 (August 1897): 194–98.

The original essay articulating DuBois' "double consciousness" theory; assign to students at all levels.

Fisher, Rudolph. "The Promised Land." *The Atlantic*, January 1927, 37–45.

A short story by African-American physician and writer, depicting life in a Harlem apartment. Assign this story alongside Ellington's *Harlem Airshaft*; access this work without a paywall or subscription at: https://www.theatlantic.com/magazine/archive/1927/01/the-promised-land/649339/.

Gioia, Ted. *The History of Jazz*. 3rd ed. Oxford University Press, 2021. https://doi.org/10.1093/oso/9780190087210.001.0001.

A comprehensive history of jazz; Chapter 3 ("Harlem," pp. 111–60) focuses on the rise of Harlem and the Harlem Renaissance, concluding with Ellington's role in developing the jazz orchestra (naming James Reese Europe and others as precursors). The introductory section of the chapter discusses the challenges faced by Harlem as a neighborhood (which the author calls "the two Harlems") despite artistic, intellectual idealism developed there. The entire book, or select chapters, would be appropriate for background reading assignments at all levels.

Kirschke, Amy Helene, ed. *Women Artists of the Harlem Renaissance*. Jackson: University Press of Mississippi, 2014. https://doi.org/10.14325/mississippi/9781628460339.001.0001.

The "Introduction" (pp. xi–xix) provides background on the central aesthetic concerns of the Harlem Renaissance, using perspectives from W.E.B. DuBois and Alain Locke, while the first chapter ("Harlem and the Renaissance: 1920–1940," pp. 3–21 by Cary D. Wintz) provides a historical overview of the movement through art, literature, and music. Both sections would be useful for building lecture material; the first chapter would be an accessible reading assignment for students.

Augusta Savage

Jenkins, Earnestine, and Kevin Sharp. *Black Artists in America: From the Great Depression to Civil Rights*. Memphis, TN, New Haven, CT: Dixon Gallery and Gardens; Yale University Press, 2021. https://www.aaeportal.com/?id=-22563.

An accessible, richly illustrated book that includes an exhibition catalogue. Chapter 2 ("Augusta Savage in Paris: African Themes and the Black Female Body," pp. 97–119) discusses Savage's background, tracing her artistic development during the period leading up to her 1939 sculpture *Lift Every Voice and Sing/The Harp*. The chapter also discusses the origins of the Harlem Renaissance movement and the idea of the "New Negro." Detailed footnotes direct readers to additional scholarship on the portrayal of Blackness in American and European art. Bring images into class, showing the multi-faceted approaches used by artists to represent Black identities within the Harlem Renaissance period.

Miah, Suejona, Asli Ali, and Natalie Nixon. "The Harp." Digital exhibition. *The Body Is Memory: An Exhibition of Black Women Artists*, 2019. https://sophia.smith.edu/afr111-f19/the-harp/.

Provides background on Savage and her sculpture, with recordings of the song that inspired it, "Lift Every Voice and Sing" by James Weldon Johnson (1871-1938). Other pages in the exhibition discuss Johnson's song, considered the "Black National Anthem." A digital exhibit created by undergraduate students, this site could be assigned as a model for a group research project (Case Study 11).

Smithsonian American Art Museum. "Augusta Savage." Digital exhibition. Accessed September 20, 2022. https://americanart.si.edu/artist/augusta-savage-4269.

Provides an overview of Savage's career (with more detail than the Miah et al. above), with links to additional works by the artist that are housed in the Smithsonian collection.

Includes photos of the artist at work. Pair this website with Miah et al. above as a short reading assignment in instances where instructors have limited time to discuss art in class.

Palmer Hayden

Mahady, Anne. "Envisioning the American Folk in the Work of Palmer C. Hayden." PhD diss., Indiana University, 2021. https://www.proquest.com/docview/2572551773/fulltextPDF/A3571793C0594D6EPQ/1?accountid=11620.

This recent dissertation may be the only full-length study on the artist Palmer Hayden. The first chapter ("Folk Things," pp. 1–36) is an excellent introduction to the aesthetic influences between folk culture in art and music in Hayden's own work, and in the Harlem Renaissance period. This chapter would be useful for an instructor wishing to place Ellington's music into an interdisciplinary context for lecture; knowledge from this chapter would also help instructors be able to shape responses to students' interpretations of music and art from this period during class discussion.

Romare Bearden

O'Meally, Robert. *Antagonistic Cooperation: Jazz, Collage, Fiction, and the Shaping of African American Culture*. Columbia University Press, 2022. https://doi.org/10.7312/omea18918.

Chapter 3 ("The 'Open Corner' of Black Community and Creativity," pp. 86–116) contextualizes several paintings by Romare Bearden (1911–1988), who was greatly influenced by Duke Ellington and other Black creatives, such as Ralph Ellison, Zora Neale Hurston, and Billie Holiday. The chapter is a wonderful introduction to early- and mid-twentieth-century African-American aesthetics; assign this chapter either as an interdisciplinary reading at all levels, or use it as a lecture-building component for instructors.

———. "'We Used to Say Stashed': Romare Bearden Paints the Blues." *Studies in the History of Art*, Symposium Papers XLVIII: Romare Bearden, American Modernist 71 (2011): 59–87.

Discusses the blues- and jazz-infused style of artist Romare Bearden, and his relationship to music and musicians. Includes several quotations about the artist by well-known commentators such as Albert Murray and Ralph Ellison. The color reproductions of several art works are very useful for class lecture material, or for student assignments. Create a short writing project or research paper asking students to do additional reading on one or two of Bearden's paintings, creating a comparative analysis with one or more Duke Ellington jazz compositions.

Duke Ellington

Ellington, Duke. *The Duke Ellington Reader*. Edited by Mark Tucker. New York: Oxford University Press, 1993. https://search.alexanderstreet.com/lti/view/work/bibliographic_entity%7Cbibliographic_details%7C4387217.

An important resource, this book includes writings and interviews by Duke Ellington on various aspects of music, race, and his career. For instructional purposes, reading excerpts from this book would introduce students to primary source work, and open analytical pathways for Ellington's music (including the music of his contemporaries). (Box 5.2.)

Boyer, Richard O. "The Hot Bach—I." *The New Yorker*, June 24, 1944. https://www.newyorker.com/magazine/1944/06/24/the-hot-bach-i.

This article is one of a three-part series on Duke Ellington that follows his career while he travels by train, performing throughout the U.S. The author intersperses historical detail with musical commentary, and fragments of interviews featuring Ellington and his band mates. It is a fascinating window into a moment in time. (See Box 5.2.) Installments two and three are also available online:

Boyer, Richard O. "The Hot Bach–II." *The New Yorker*, July 1, 1944. https://archives.newyorker.com/newyorker/1944-07-01/flipbook/026/.

Boyer, Richard O. "The Hot Bach–III." *The New Yorker*, July 8, 1944. https://archives.newyorker.com/newyorker/1944-07-08/flipbook/026/.

Green, Edward, ed. *The Cambridge Companion to Duke Ellington*. 1st ed. Cambridge University Press, 2014. https://doi.org/10.1017/CCO9781139021357.

An indispensable resource on the composer, including many biographical and analytical articles suitable for reading assignments at any level.

Malcolm, Douglass. "'Myriad Subtleties': Subverting Racism through Irony in the Music of Duke Ellington and Dizzy Gillespie." *Black Music Research Journal* 35, no. 2 (2015): 185–227.

A lengthy article, this reading would be most suitable for graduate students as an assignment. Instructors can use the wealth of background information on Duke Ellington, his piece "Black and Tan Fantasy," the Cotton Club, signifying, and other African-American musico-cultural practices to build an engaging lecture.

Metzer, David. "Shadow Play: The Spiritual in Duke Ellington's 'Black and Tan Fantasy.'" *Black Music Research Journal* 17, no. 2 (1997): 137–58.

Instructors could build an entire module on African-American music and culture based on this article alone. I recommend assigning all the musical and textual references in chronological order (with corollary readings) to give students the "long century" background that they need to be able to study the jazz piece "Black and Tan Fantasy" by Ellington, and the film *Black and Tan* (1929), which could serve as a capstone to the whole module. Instructors could then assign this article (which is accessible even to undergraduates) as the final reading. It would be an interesting "experiment" to assign this article both at the beginning and end of the module to discover how much more students were able to gain from the article at the end (hopefully inspiring advanced students to listen while reading to practice active engagement with scholarly content). Students could write a brief reflection on what they understood to be the most important layers of information after the first and second readings; then have students write a brief reflection on how their appreciation of Ellington changed with additional background knowledge.

Murray, Albert. "Storiella Americana as She Is Swyung: Duke Ellington, the Culture of Washington, D.C. and the Blues as Representative Anecdote." *Conjunctions*, The Music Issue 16 (1991): 209–19.

Although this is an older article, I recommend it highly for its accessibility and writing flair (not to mention the author's status in the Black community as literary critic). The article describes the musical and social environments that impacted Ellington's career, while explaining in simple terms the jazz forms that he utilized. Finally, the author argues for the quintessential "Americanness" of Ellington's music, which would be helpful for instructors wanting to make the case that *Harlem Airshaft* should be included in our discussions of musical nationalism (alongside other works that depict American landscapes).

Murray, Albert. "The Vernacular Imperative: Duke Ellington's Place in the National Pantheon." *Callaloo* 14, no. 4 (1991): 771–75.

A brief article reflecting on the importance of Ellington—and the importance of monuments—in music historiography. This piece would be very helpful for a reading assignment when instructors wish to discuss how canons form, how composers enter the canon, and why we gravitate towards "monuments" to tell historical narratives.

Analytical Frameworks

Burrows, George. "'Black, Brown and Beige' and the Politics of Signifyin(g)." *Jazz Research Journal* 1, no. 1 (2007): 45–71.

Assign this article for advanced students; Burrows discusses the polemics of categories (based on Foucault), Ellington's approaches to musical genre and trickster narratives, and provides a discursive musical analysis according to the signifying framework of *Black, Brown, and Beige*. For survey classes, instructors could use the analytical section as a lecture-building component guiding students on how to listen to and interpret jazz.

Floyd, Samuel A. *The Power of Black Music: Interpreting Its History from Africa to the United States*. 1. iss. as paperback. Oxford Paperbacks. New York: Oxford University Press, 1996.

A formative book for studying African-American music, it includes several detailed analyses that can help instructors and students "hear" jazz at a critical level, and recognize the signifying processes often present. Chapter 4 focuses on signifying ("African-American Modernism, Signifyin(g), and Black Music," 87–99), and would be a more accessible reading assignment than the Gates (below); Chapter 5 focuses on the Harlem and Chicago Renaissance movements and has several passages on Ellington ("The Negro Renaissance: Harlem and Chicago Flowerings," pp. 130–35).

Gates, Henry Louis. *The Signifying Monkey: A Theory of African-American Literary Criticism*. 1. Oxford University Press paperback. Oxford Paperbacks. New York, NY: Oxford University Press, 1989.

This is the classic text that first identified signifying as a theoretical framework and narrative strategy in African-American literature. It is a challenging read since it not only assumes knowledge of the literature discussed, but also uses vocabulary and ways of explaining things that can be dense for undergraduate readers. I recommend this book for graduate students needing to use the theory for their own advanced research projects, and for any instructors needing to become more familiar with the idea or who wish to make literary comparisons for teaching purposes.

Maxile, Horace J. "Signs, Symphonies, Signifyin(G): African-American Cultural Topics as Analytical Approach to the Music of Black Composers." *Black Music Research Journal*, Becoming: Blackness and the Musical Imagination 28, no. 1 (2008): 123–38.

Maxile's article provides a broad overview of the topic of signifying in African-American music criticism, with a detailed reading of Frederick Tillis' work *Freedom* (1996)—which makes a great listening assignment alongside this article; Maxile discusses ways that this analytical strategy might apply to jazz. To create a mini-module on signifying in African-American music, assign the Smith "Blues, Criticism" (below) on a class day prior to class day(s) on Ellington; follow up with the Maxile afterwards. Maxile also includes helpful bibliography on the development of the idea of signifying within African-American music, for instructors, researchers, and graduate students who might want to incorporate this methodology into their musicological work.

Smith, Ayana. "Blues, Criticism, and the Signifying Trickster." *Popular Music* 24, no. 2, Literature and Music (2005): 179–91.

This article argues for signifying as both a narrative musical strategy, and as a performative identity in the early blues repertory. As a reading assignment for all levels, the detailed examples will give students a deeper understanding of how signifying applies to musical compositional processes. For instructors wishing to use the "long century" approach to African-American music, develop a unit (or several classes) on blues, its origins, development, and musical style.

Index

American Indians *see* Indigenous Americans
appropriation: cultural 33, 59, 75–77, 86, 88; musical 60, 76*b*, 82*b*, 88, 89; *see also* cultural extractivism; Indianist movement; musical borrowing
archives: of African-American folksong 66; of Indigenous American musics 90, 91; in pedagogical contexts 58*b*, 60–61*b*, 82; *see also* primary sources
authenticity: in compositional voice 76*b*, 82*b*; in cultural representation 34, 76*b*, 82*b*, 86; in filmic portrayals 87; in performance practice 56, 72; *see also* intercultural; transcultural

Beach, Amy Marcy Cheney 11, *65*, 75–89; and American musical nationalism 78, 82, 86; and birdsong 78, 79, 84, 86; in Europe 78; and George Whitefield Chadwick 78, 83*b*, 86; and landscape 77, 79, 81–82, 85; and Native American melodies 75, 77, 78–83*b*, 85–89; and nature 84, 86; as a prodigy 78; as a symphonic composer 78–79; *see also* appropriation; musical borrowing
Beach, Amy Marcy Cheney, musical works by: *From Blackbird Hills* 75, 80; *Gaelic Symphony* 77, 78, 89; "Hermit Thrush at Eve" 79; "Hermit Thrush at Morn" 77, 79, 86; *String Quartet* 75–77, 79–80, 83*b*, 85, 87–89
Bearden, Romare 101
blackface 44, 93*b*; as analogy in scholarship 86; in Europe 48*b*, 56, 72–73; in minstrelsy 44, 56, 72–73, 93*b*; *see also* minstrelsy
Bloom's Taxonomy *2*; *see also* pedagogical tools
blues: aesthetics and style 71, 74, 92, 93, 101, 103, 104; electric 57, 66–68*b*; folk 29, 30, 38
Boas, Franz 80, 87, 90; "The Central Eskimo" 87; *see also* ethnology
borrowing *see* musical borrowing

cakewalk 11, 29, 58–59*b*; in musical works by: (Florence Price 57, 61; Will Marion Cook 93)
Caldara, Antonio (1670-1736) 5*b*, 16
Casulana, Maddalena 20*b*, 37, 38
Chadwick, George Whitefield: and Amy Beach 78, 83*b*, 86; and Florence Price 64, 65*b*
Chicago World's Fair (1933) 61; *see also* Tennessee Centennial Exposition; New York World's Fair; World's Columbian Exposition
civil rights movements 62, 63*b*, 67, 68; and Black Artists 100; Booker T. Washington and 96; and Florence Price 57, 62, 63*b*; and the Harlem Renaissance 97; Muddy Waters and 67–68; and slavery 24

Index

Cleopatra VII Philopator 23; representations of 23, 26–28, 46
Cook, Will Marion 93–94*b*; Musical works by: (*Clorindy/The First Cakewalk* 93*b*; *In Dahomey* 93–94*b*)
core repertory: in syllabus design 3, 9, 10, 13; *see also* pedagogical tools
critical/analytical (reasons for inclusion) 2, 8–10, 13; *see also* pedagogical tools
critical race theory (CRT) 33, 40–41*b*, 70–71; *see also* hypervisibility
cultural extractivism 54, 80, 85, 90; and ethnology 80; *see also* appropriation; Indianist movement

Danger Mouse [Burton, Brian] 18, 21–22, 37
Davids, Brent Michael 13, 75, 76, 83–84, 88–90; and American musical nationalism 76; musical works by: (*By Our Nature* 83–84, 90; Lutheran chorale tune 88; *Welcome to PauWau* 88–89, 90)
Des Prez, Josquin 18, 22, 37–38
double consciousness 59*b*, 92, 93, 95–99; *see also* long century of African-American music
DuBois, W.E.B. 39, 71, 96–98, 99, 100; double consciousness theory of 59*b*, 92, 93, 95–99; educational philosophy of 39, 68, 71
Dvořák, Antonín 11, 78, 83*b*, 86; and American musical nationalism 11, 86

Ellington, Duke 11, 16, 95*b*, 93–99, 101–3; and American musical nationalism 16, 103; comparison to Bach 102; participation in the Great Migration 99; primary sources on 102; as symphonic composer 98; *see also* Harlem Renaissance

Ellington, Duke, musical works by: *Black and Tan* (film score) 94*b*, 102; "Black and Tan Fantasy" 102; *Black, Brown, and Beige* 103; "Echoes of Harlem" 94; *Harlem* 16, 98; *Harlem Airshaft* 16, 94–98; "Harlem River Quiver" 94; "Harlem Speaks" 94
Ellison, Ralph 40, 101; *see also* Harlem Renaissance
ethnology: and collecting 80; and cultural extractivism 80; displays of, at World's Fairs and Expositions 81–82*b*, 88; and the Indianist movement 88; and land allotment 75, 80, 81, 88; and transcription of Indigenous American melodies 75, 80, 83*b*, 86–87, 90, 91; *see also* cultural extractivism; Indianist movement
exoticism 40–43, 45–46, 59*b*; definition of 23, 25, 38, 45; in opera 8, 9, 18, 23, 26–27, 38, 46; *see also* Mimesis to Mockery
extractivism *see* cultural extractivism

Fisk University 66; Fisk Jubilee Singers of 41*b*
Fletcher, Alice Cunningham 80–82, 87, 88, 90; influence of on Amy Beach 81–82; and land allotment 80–81, 88; *A Study of Omaha Indian Music* 80, 87; at the World's Columbian Exposition 81; *see also* ethnology

Gabrieli, Giovanni 6*b*, 14
Gershwin, George 29, 32–35, 76*b*, 89; primary sources on 33, 34
Gershwin, George, musical works by: *Porgy and Bess* 29, 32–35, 76*b*
Great Migration, the: composers participating in: (Duke Ellington 99; Florence Price 57, 64, 68*b*, Muddy Waters 57, 68*b*; historical narratives of 62, 96, 99; influence

Index   107

on the blues 68; represented in music 67b, 68b, 99); see also Harlem Renaissance
Guidonian hand 19b, 20

Handel, George Frideric 5b, 7–10, 18, 23–28, 38, 46, 47
Handel, George Frideric, musical works by: Works: (*Giulio Cesare* 8, 10, 18, 23–28, 38, 46, 47; *Messiah* 8, 10; *Rodrigo, ovvero Vincer se stesso è la maggio vittoria*, 5b)
Harlem Renaissance 10, 11, 18, 33, 57, 60, 67b, 68b, 95–101, 103; see also Great Migration; New Negro, the
Hayden, Palmer 97, 101; see also Harlem Renaissance
hexachord 18, 19–21b
Hughes, Langston 67, 94; see also Harlem Renaissance
Hurston, Zora Neale 96, 101; see also Harlem Renaissance
hypervisibility 40, *41*, 42–45, 50, 52, 54; see also critical race theory; stereotypes

identity: definitions of, in Europe 18, 24; and double consciousness of 97; ethnic and racial 24–25, *41*; segmentation of, in early modern Venice 14, 15; stereotypes 17, *41*, 88; see also double consciousness; identity, representation of
identity, representation of *41*, 42–47; in baroque drama 5b, 23–29, 38, 50, 53b; in instrumental music 80; in modern performances 55, 104; in primary sources 25, 45, 47, 52, 56, 57; in Sephardic romances 5b; in works by: (Amy Beach 90; Brent Michael Davids 89; George Gershwin 32–34, 89; Florence Price 60, 89; Muddy Waters 67, 74; William Grant Still 10, 89; at Worlds' Fairs 82b); see also hypervisibility; language; Mimesis to Mockery; origin myth; stereotypes
Indianist movement 74, 77, 79, 83b, 86, 88; influenced by ethnology 88; see also appropriation; cultural extractivism
Indigenous Americans, musical borrowing from: 73, 75–83b, 85, 86; as a project of American musical nationalism 73, 76, 77
Indigenous Americans, representations of: 23, 24, 44, 71, 73, 86, 88; at the Chicago World's Columbian Exposition 81, 82b; in classroom instruction 47–56; in music by Jean Philippe Rameau 47–48, 50–56, 71–72
Indigenous Americans: archives of music by 90, 91; cultural artifacts of 80, 81b, 82; curatorial relationships with 81b; ethnologies of 75, 80, 81, 86–87; and land allotment 80–81, 86–88; musical historiography of 77; musics by 16, 75, 82b, 84, 88–91; in Paris 49; primary sources regarding 81, 83b, 85–87; song cultures of 82; see also Davids, Brent Michael; La Flesche, Frances
intercultural: perspectives in pedagogy 9; practices in Indigenous communities 90; voice in composition 75, 76b, 83; see also authenticity; transcultural
intersectional/historical (reasons for inclusion) 2, 3, 9–10, 12–13; see also pedagogical tools
invisibility 40, *41*, 42–45, 50, 52; see also critical race theory

Jacquet de la Guerre, Élisabeth Claude 48b, 49b, 58b
Johnson, Robert 66–67b
Joplin, Scott 18, 29–33b, 38–39, 57

juba dance 11, 59b–60, 74; in minstrelsy 60; in musical works by Florence Price 59b–60, 73–74
just in time teaching, 32; *see also* pedagogical tools

La Flesche, Francis 86, 87; *Ka-Me-Ha*: (*The Omaha Stories of Francis La Flesche* 87); *see also* ethnology
language: describing race or ethnicity 23–25, 28, 34, 57; sensitive and harmful 23–23, 36–37, 71; *see also* identity, representation of
layered pathway 6–7, 11, 13, 18, 33b, 50, 82, 91, *94*, 98; *see also* pedagogical tools
Like the Light of Liberty: in classroom instruction 11, 82b, 93–94b; definition 85, 93; as framework for analysis 11, 85, 92–94; *see also* research methodologies
liturgy 4b, 6b, 12, 14–15, 18; Catholic 12, 14, 18; Jewish 4b, 6b, 15
Locke, Alain 96–98, 100; *see also* Harlem Renaissance; New Negro, the
Locke, Ralph (musicologist) 38, 45; *see also* exoticism
Lomax, Alan (folklorist and ethnomusicologist) 30, 66
long century of African-American music: in classroom contexts 98, 102, 104; definition of 92–93; *see also* research methodologies
Lully, Jean-Baptiste 48b, 71, 73

mashup 17, 18, 21–22, 37
mimesis 40–47, 51–52, 54, 55, 58b; *see also* Mimesis to Mockery
Mimesis to Mockery:in classroom instruction 7–9, 46–47, 51–52; 54–55, 58–59b, 86–87; definition 7–9, 40, *41*; as framework for analysis 8–9, 40, *41*, 42–43, 45–47, 54–55, 57; in historical narratives 45–47; *see also* exoticism; hypervisibility; mimesis; research methodologies; stereotypes
minstrelsy 57, 58, 59b, 60, 93–94b; blackface in 44, 56, 73, 86, 93b; in Europe 11, 72; stereotypes in 35, 72, 93b
modes, musical 4, 15, 19b, 42
Monteverdi, Claudio 5, 42, 92
motet 4, 12, 17–23, 37–38
musical borrowing 21–22, 37, 67, 75–77b, 86, 89; of African-American music 11; of Indigenous American musics 77, 79, 83b, 86; in motets 22; *see also* appropriation; mashup; intercultural; quotation; transcultural

nationalism: in the baroque era 5, 8, 9, 72
nationalism, in the U.S.: as defined by borrowing Indigenous American musics 73, 76, 77; as defined by the Second New England School 78; at Fairs and Expositions 82b, 86; and jazz 11; in music by Aaron Copland 11; in music by African-American composers 73; in music by Amy Beach 78, 82, 86; in music by Antonín Dvořák 11, 86; in music by Brent Michael Davids 76; in music by Duke Ellington 16, 103; in music by Florence Price 66; regarding land and landscape 16, 76, 87, 89
Native Americans *see* Indigenous Americans
New Negro, the 60, 96–98, 100; *see also* Harlem Renaissance; Locke, Alain
New York World's Fair (1939) 97; *see also* Chicago World's Fair;

Tennessee Centennial Exposition; World's Columbian Exposition

orchestra, composer(s) for: American 65*b*; Amy Beach as 78; Duke Ellington as 95, 100; Florence Price as 60, 61, 65*b*; George Frideric Handel as 10; jazz 92, 95, 100; Jean-Philippe Rameau as 47; William Grant Still as 10; women as 65*b*; *see also* symphony, composer(s) of the

orientalism 23, 45, 76, 86; *see also* postcolonialism; Said, Edward

origin myth: definition of 17–19, 35n3; as framework for analysis 7–10, 15, 17, 33, 36, 47; in historical narratives 17–19, 25, 29, 33–35, 43, 45–47, 50, 68, 77, 87, 95; *see also* shadow history; stereotypes

Origin Myths and Shadow Histories 7–10, 15, 33, 36, 47; *see also* origin myth; research methodologies

pedagogical tools: Bloom's taxonomy 2; critical/analytical (reasons for inclusion) 2, 8–10, 13; intersectional/historical (reasons for inclusion) 2, 3, 9–10, 12–13; just in time teaching 32; layered pathway 6–7, 11, 13, 18, 33*b*, 50, 82, 91, *94*, 98; sensitive and harmful language 23–25, 36–37, 71; shift in thinking 7, 9–13, 17–19, 47, 50, 98; ticket to enter 31–32, 95*b*

Pollarolo, Carlo Francesco 5*b*, 15

postcolonialism 23, 36, 43, 45, 46, 77; *see also* Said, Edward

Price, Florence 57–66, 73–74; and African-American History 63*b*; and American musical nationalism 66; and the Civil Rights Movement 57, 62, 63*b*; compared to William Grant Still 83; and George Whitefield Chadwick 64, 65*b*; and the Great Migration 57, 64, 68*b*; and the Harlem Renaissance 57, 60; and primary sources 73–74; and racial violence 63; representations of identity in music by 56–57, 60, 89, 93–94*b*; and signifying 57, 58, 59*b*; social and political issues impacting the life of 62–64; and syllabus design 65–66*b*; *see also* cakewalk; Great Migration; Harlem Renaissance; juba dance

Price, Florence, musical works by: analysis of 58, 59*b*, 60, 68; and the cakewalk 58, 60; *Dances in the Canebrakes* 57–66, 68; and the Harlem Renaissance 68; and the juba dance 59*b*–60, 73–74; *Piano Concerto in One Movement* 61; and signifying 57, 58–59*b*; "Silk Hat and Walking Cane" 58–60, 74; symbolism in 57; *Symphony in E Minor*: (and the Chicago World's Fair 61; and the juba dance 60; and teaching strategies 61–62, 73); and vernacular gestures 57

primary sources: on African Americans 56, 92, 94, 102; on Duke Ellington 102; on Florence Price 73–74; on George Gershwin 33, 34; on Indigenous Americans 50–52, 57, 81, 83*b*, 85–87; in pedagogy and student research 33, 34, 51, 60–61*b*, 61–62, 83*b*, 94; representations of identity and stereotypes in 25, 45, 47, 52, 56, 57; *see also* archives; pedagogical tools

prodigies: women as 49*b*, 78

quotation: of folksong 79; of Indigenous American musics 75–77, 79, 82, 83, 87, 89; of pre-existing music 21; *see also* musical borrowing

Rameau, Jean-Philippe 28, 47–57, 71–72, 87; as composer for orchestra 47; representations of Indigenous Americans by 47–48, 50–56, 71–72

Rameau, Jean-Philippe, musical works by: *Les indes galantes* 28, 47, 52; "Les Sauvages"/*Les Sauvages* 47–48, 50–53, 56–57, 71–72, 87; *Nouvelles suites* 47, 50–52

research methodologies: critical race theory 33, 40–41b, 70–71; double consciousness 59b, 92, 93, 95–99; invisibility/hypervisibility 40, *41*, 42–45, 50, 52, 54; Like the Light of Liberty: (in classroom contexts 98, 102, 104; in classroom instruction 11, 82b, 93–94b; definition 85, 93; as framework for analysis 11, 85, 92–94; long century of African-American music definition of 92–93); Mimesis to Mockery: (definition 7–9, 40–41; in classroom instruction 7–9, 46–47, 51–52, 54–55, 58–59b, 86–87; as framework for analysis 8–9, 40–43, 45–47, 54–55, 57; in historical narratives 45–46; Origin Myths and Shadow Histories 7–10, 15, 33, 36, 47; signifying 21, 22, 57, 59b, 67b, 74, 92–94b, 98, 102–104)

ring shout 29, 38, 39, 59b

Rossi, Salamone 5, 6; musical works by: (*Ha-shirim asher lishlomo* (*The Songs of Solomon*), 6)

Said, Edward 23, 36; *see also* postcolonialism

Savage, Augusta 97, 100–101; *see also* Harlem Renaissance

sensitive and harmful language 23–25, 36–37, 71; *see also* pedagogical tools

Sephardic songs 5b, 15

shadow history: definition of 9; as framework for analysis 7–10, 15, 33, 36, 47, 57; in historical narratives 17–19, 22, 25, 29, 43, 45–47, 68, 77, 87, 95; as pedagogical tool 8, 17–19, 22, 33–34b, 47, 50, 76–77; *see also* origin myth; Origin Myths and Shadow Histories

shift in thinking 7, 9–13, 17–19, 47, 50, 98; *see also* pedagogical tools

signifying 21, 22, 57, 59b, 67b, 74, 92–94b, 98, 102–4; *see also* research methodologies

signifying trickster, the 74, 93, 104; narratives of: (in musical works by Duke Ellington 103; in musical works by Muddy Waters 67); *see also* research methodologies

sol-fa 18, 19b, 20b

Spain: and colonialism 50; expulsion of Moors from 5; representations of, in French opera 53, 54; representations of, in Italian opera 5b, 15–16; in Sephardic songs 5b

stereotypes 10, 42–46, 64, 75, 77, 84, 87, 90; in historical narratives 17, 50, 95; in minstrelsy 35, 72, 93b; in modern performances 9, 34–35, 55; in musical representations 22, 26–28, 33, 51, 54, 57, 72, 88; of the "noble savage" 54, 72, 82; pedagogical strategies to address 35, 58–59b, 65b, 74, 87; in primary sources 9, 34, 45, 47, 52, 56, 57, 86; *see also* hypervisibility; minstrelsy; origin myth

Still, William Grant 10–13, 16, 33b, 62b, 64–65b, 83, 86, 89, 95–96; *see also* Harlem Renaissance

Still, William Grant, musical works by: *Afro-American Symphony* 10, 62b; *Darker America* 11; *Kaintuck* 11, 16, 86; *Lenox Avenue* 16; *Levee Land* 11; *Seven Traceries* 11, 14 symphony, composer(s) of the: African American 64, 73–74, 104; Amy Beach as 77–79; Duke Ellington as 98; Florence Price as 60–62; William Grant Still as 10; women as 64, 74; *see also* individual composers, musical works by; orchestra, composer(s) for

Tennessee Centennial Exposition (1897) 82*b*
think-pair-share 27, 51, 95*b*; *see also* pedagogical tools
ticket to enter 31–32, 95*b*; *see also* pedagogical tools
transcultural: perspectives in pedagogy 88, 89; voice in composition 39, 83, 89; *see also* authenticity; intercultural

Varèse, Edgard 10–11, 64
Von Glahn, Denise (musicologist) 16, 65*b*, 74, 78, 85, 86

Washington, Booker T. 39, 96
Waters, Muddy 57, 66–68*b*, 74; commercial success of 66; and the Great Migration 57, 68*b*; and the Harlem Renaissance 68; influence on rock by 66–67
Waters, Muddy, musical works by: "Country Blues" 66, 67*b*; "I Feel Like Going Home" 66, 67*b*; "Mannish Boy" 57, 66–68, 74; and civil rights 67–68*b*
World's Columbian Exposition (1893) 81–82*b*, 85, 86, 88; *see also* Chicago World's Fair; New York World's Fair; Tennessee Centennial Exposition

Taylor & Francis eBooks

www.taylorfrancis.com

A single destination for eBooks from Taylor & Francis with increased functionality and an improved user experience to meet the needs of our customers.

90,000+ eBooks of award-winning academic content in Humanities, Social Science, Science, Technology, Engineering, and Medical written by a global network of editors and authors.

TAYLOR & FRANCIS EBOOKS OFFERS:

- A streamlined experience for our library customers
- A single point of discovery for all of our eBook content
- Improved search and discovery of content at both book and chapter level

REQUEST A FREE TRIAL
support@taylorfrancis.com

Milton Keynes UK
Ingram Content Group UK Ltd.
UKHW031328071224
451979UK00004B/19